TO
LOSE
A
WAR

Villa Fürstenhof

TO LOSE A WAR

Memories of a German Girl

Regina Maria Shelton

Southern Illinois University Press
Carbondale and Edwardsville

Library of Congress Cataloging in Publication Data

Shelton, Regina Maria, 1927–
    To lose a war.

    1. Shelton, Regina Maria, 1927– . 2. World War, 1939–1945—
Personal narratives, German.   3. Silesia—Biography.   I. Title.
D811.5.S484   1982   940.54'82'43   82-5916
ISBN 0-8093-1074-0   AACR2
Printed in the United States of America
Edited by Joyce Atwood
Designed by Quentin Fiore
Illustrated by Millie Dunkel
Production supervised by John DeBacher

85 84 83 82   5 4 3 2 1

Wer nie sein Brot mit Tränen aß,
Wer nie die kummervollen Nächte
Auf seinem Bette weinend saß,
Der kennt euch nicht, ihr himmlischen Mächte.
JOHANN WOLFGANG VON GOETHE,
Harfenspieler

How short our happy days appear!
How long the sorrowful!
JEAN INGELOW, *The Mariner's Cave*, St. 38.

Come what come may,
Time and the hour runs through the roughest day.
SHAKESPEARE, *Macbeth*, Act i, sc. 3, l. 146.

Contents

Illustrations

Acknowledgments

To the few persons who knew of my undertaking I owe a special debt of gratitude:

Thomas E. Cassidy, Emeritus of English, Southern Illinois University at Carbondale, who acted as the only confidant in the early stages of writing and whose enthusiasm lent momentum to the initial attempt.

E. Earle Stibitz, Emeritus of English, Southern Illinois University at Carbondale, who devoted himself to the tedious details of critical reading and who remained patient and ever sensitive to my idiosyncrasies, offering his expertise and support in every way.

Marianne Beck, who shared with me many of the trying experiences of our youth and who relinquished to me her personal diaries to supplement and corroborate my own.

William E. Shelton, who insisted that this book be written and who encouraged me in his fashion along the way.

My sons, who respected my need for solitude and who with me eagerly awaited the outcome of my efforts.

I dedicate this book to the memory of those who wittingly or unwittingly shaped my life and who now populate these pages, and to the memory of my homeland, Silesia.

REGINA MARIA SHELTON

Prologue

My cousin Hans in West Germany is a genealogy buff who pursues his hobby with fervor and admirable thoroughness. Less than half an hour ago we arrived at his house, my son Tom and I, and are now seated comfortably on the terrace. On one side it is sheltered by the house wall with a large picture window of the winter garden where cacti and tropical plants thrive protected year round; at a rectangle an open fireplace that wards off the cold on days more inclement than today forms the wall to the street side. We look out over the goldfish pond and the flower-bordered lawn of the quiet back yard. His wife, Helga, is busy preparing the afternoon coffee, leaving Hans and me to chat leisurely and become attuned to each other again after years of separation.

"We might as well get down to business while we have the time," says Hans as he excuses himself to go into the house. He returns with several thick three-ring binders and a sheaf of loose forms. I leaf through the pages of one of the volumes until some names as familiar as my own catch my eye. They draw me into the past that is here recorded in meticulous entries in typescript, enhanced by inserts of photocopied documents in the stilted, careful penmanship of long-dead public officials and priests, and even by some pictures restored through photoduplication. Hans tolerates my reverie long enough to let me catch the mood of his own fascination before he spreads a clean form on the table and begins questioning me for names and dates and relationships. And I dredge my memory, pleased at the gleam in his eyes when some data form hesitantly on my lips that have eluded him so far or needed confirmation. He takes notes, then reaches for other sheets to make entries on them, to link them eventually into the web of ancestry which he is reconstructing and in which our origins are rooted. Genealogy—that is how they started, Hans's trips behind the Iron Curtain, in search of forefathers whose land was pulled from under us like a slippery rug when we were young, and in search of our homeland's history that we only learned to cherish when a foreign people claimed it as their own.

We are on the eve of a journey to Silesia, the region east of the Oder-Neisse line, Polish territory since the end of World War II. For me it will be the first encounter with places I had known so well over thirty years ago and had left aboard a freight train, a lonely, frightened girl among hundreds of homeless in equal misery and desolation. As the years passed and turned the girl into a graying woman, the child in me clamored to go home.

Is this moving day? The entrance hall is lined with baggage— a few suitcases, many cardboard boxes, bundles wrapped in plastic, picnic hampers. Helga had been packing deep into the previous night and stands in the kitchen early this morning amidst a clutter of thermos jugs, sausages, fruit, and a basket of still warm breakfast buns.

"How will we get all this in the van?" She surveys her violated house with a despairing gesture.

"We'll manage. Just get the food ready," comes the response from Hans, who is concentrating on his list of gifts and provisions. "Camera and films, tape recorder and tapes, ointment for Julia, the mixer for the pastor—what about Grandpa's overcoat, have you packed that already?"

While I spread butter and sausage on the buns, I listen in

amazement to the items being checked off the list and see yet more bundles being carried to the stacks in the hallway.

"They are grateful for everything we can take them, you will see. No, you can't possibly imagine what it's like until you see for yourself," says Helga to me with a mirthless chuckle as she fills the thermos bottles with steaming coffee. She is too busy to be asked the many questions of who and why that are on my mind. I know that none of our relatives and friends have remained in Silesia; all of them shared the fate as expellees at approximately the same time in 1946. For whom, then, are the canned goods, the appliances, the medications? For strangers? For the enemies who disowned us? Why this lavish care, this thoughtful anticipation of their needs? I look at Hans who is a man of moderate means and at his mop of prematurely white hair: His life has been work and worry and risk-taking on his professional climb. I look at Helga and the worry lines on her forehead and the hands that speak of hard work in the service of her family of three growing sons. What makes them want to care and share with strangers? I feel intimidated by their concerns, which I do not understand, and suspect that I have much to learn.

The notion of this trip, which I had planned for purely selfish motives to indulge my sentimentality, becomes unhinged and uncomfortably confused. After weeks of traveling in West Germany and enjoying luxuries and impeccable cleanliness everywhere, what kind of vacation lies ahead for Tom and me?

"This is positively the last time that you talk me into this ordeal," sighs Helga toward Hans as she hands him the huge Tupperware container with sandwich buns. He grins, knowing better, and goes outside to direct the loading operations.

Gradually the idea gets hold of me that this is, indeed, a moving day of sorts, moving commonplace riches of the West to another world where they will be treasures, and moving all the indispensable frills of our accustomed life style to have them available when we will be among people as yet unafflicted by our overwrought demands.

For better or worse, the adventure is about to begin.

The three teenage boys—Hans's sons Rolf and Werner, and my Tom—are pacing the courtyard, restless like race horses at the starting post. They have opened the sliding door on the side and the rear gate of the shiny orange-and-white VW-bus that Hans has rented for our expedition. Two other passengers, elderly women, are already settled on the last row of seats, equally as anxious to get started as the impatient boys.

"Everybody out! Let's get this carriage loaded systematically and see if there is room for all of you," shouts Hans cheerfully.

His mother, Helene, and Aunt Anna clear the way and sit on a garden bench while the rest of us transfer the baggage from the hallway into the courtyard and watch it disappear in the rear compartment of the van, under the seats, sleeping bags unfolded on top of the seats, and camera, tape recorder, maps stashed in the glove compartment. A last check of the kitchen and the hallway, then with a heave and a ho the bus gate slams shut.

Behind the rear seat, which I share with Helene and Anna, rises a solid wall of boxes and bundles. The boys take the middle row of seats. Rolf and Werner hand their African leather hats to us to be deposited somewhere in back—these good-luck charms they would not think of leaving behind. Hans and Helga sit in front. Before the sliding door is set in motion, Helga's ninety-three-year-old grandfather hobbles on his cane into the courtyard to inspect the touring party and shakes hands all around. He and his elderly daughter, who will care for him in our absence, stand back and wave until we roll out of sight.

We are on our way due east. Hans speaks the introduction to his taped travelogue into the microphone. I begin to jot down journal notes as soon as we leave town, determined to record at least in catchword style everything we see and experience. The morning is pleasantly cool under broken clouds. Intermittently the sun breaks through, lighting up patches of the peaceful heath around us.

"Passports up front," orders Hans, and obediently we entrust the most precious and crucial items we possess to him who will relieve us of all formalities that lie ahead. Berlin is 235 kilometers away, but the border to East Germany only three-quarters of an hour from our point of departure.

Checkpoint Alpha near Helmstedt comes into view, with West German, British, French, and United States flags hoisted high above the gate. The Stars and Stripes never meant more to me than at this moment of parting when we pass it and leave it behind. The stretch of asphalt before us fans out into a multitude of traffic lanes that are confined on both sides by high, small-meshed fences, two rows of them on each side, topped by barbed wire. Beyond the fences are guard towers.

The sight reminds me uncomfortably of the East-West border through the Harz Mountains at which Tom and I stood a short time ago, with the dividing ditch hard behind the border post, the fence, the raked and allegedly mined strip beyond, the patrol road, and the guard tower. We could see soldiers train their field glasses on us through the wooden slats, and we could see that in nearby houses the west windows were boarded up to keep their inhabitants from communicating with westerners. I also remember our visit to the West German border-guard garrison at Goslar where an officer demonstrated for us on a model the hazards of this most infamous of all borders that cuts like a festering scar for hundreds of kilometers through the heart of Germany. I detested what I heard and saw then almost like a personal violation, felt threatened by the proximity of such blatant hostility but, most of all, enraged by the brazenness of it. Now I am about to cross irrevocably into a country that appears to defy any amiable approach.

The layout of the checkpoint on the East German side is elaborate. Fifteen lanes for passenger cars and an additional seven for trucks lead to as many gates and booths. The traffic on our side is light, and we move up for the first passport control within moments. Although I knew that the soldiers would be Germans, to hear them speak and act no differently from us comes as a shock. They wear the traditional field-gray uniforms of the World War II German army. Hans is asked politely for destination and passports. We have crossed so many borders within Europe where a perfunctory wave of a passport, sometimes not even opened, produced the magic entry into another country. Not here—

"Sunglasses off! Get ready for face control," whispers Rolf who has experienced this before. In total silence we strip our faces and position ourselves to be in full view of the soldier who peers into the bus and matches each passport to the appropriate face.

Then we are rolling again. My foolishly pounding heart finds its normal rhythm again. One shouldn't believe all the stories of harassment and chicanery, I think, almost ashamed of my gullibility. Tom turns around to me with a guilty look.

"Mom, I hate to tell you, but I forgot to take the knife out of my jacket."

This time my heart skips a beat. Not five minutes ago the soldier had asked if we carried weapons, ammunition, transmitters, etc. Does Tom's switch-blade knife, his proudest possession and a gift from his German deer-hunting uncle, qualify as a weapon? I gasp and take it from him, consigning it to the bottom of the nearest food hamper, ostensibly to be explained away as a picnic knife in lieu of normal silverware on the road.

I am told that we are traveling on one of the oldest stretches of Autobahn in Germany, and at times the bumpy road convinces me that this is so. We alternate between single and double lanes leading east; others beyond a median are going west. They are all but empty in our direction. The western lanes show a spread-out but steady stream of cars, all of them with western plates. When I comment on the absence of East German vehicles, Hans explains to me that we are traversing a restricted zone where East German residents are permitted only with very special passes. Farther on I spot the first unfamiliar foreign car, foreign only to me who has never seen an East German designed "Trabant," or "Trabi" for short. In general, the road is in very good condition and shows signs of constant maintenance. I comment on this to Hans.

"Why not?" says Hans. "We are paying for it."

"You mean this is a toll road?"

"You might call it that! Since there is so much traffic between West Germany and West Berlin, our government pays a subsidy to East Germany for every West German vehicle that uses it."

There is nothing remarkable about the sights on either side. The few towns and villages we see are too distant from the road to make an impression, except that they seem to lack color, the gleaming white of fresh paint and the bright red or bluish slate of new roofs that dominate in West German scenes. The gentle roll of the land is covered with fields of harvest-golden grain and green spreads of vegetable and feed crops. To my midwestern American eye their size is not unusual until I superimpose on them the patchy look of West German farmland and realize that these fields are enormous, stretching uninterrupted for miles, it seems. They are huge collectives; combines, always several of them, working in the same area underline the impression of a concerted state effort. On some acreage where the harvest is already finished, neatly stacked house-high mounds of straw dot the landscape.

We drive under overpasses that advertise in bold signs the Leipzig fair, urge highway safety, and admonish residents to various laudable efforts in terms and acronyms almost unintelligible to the uninitiated. To my son I can point out the first real-life Russian soldiers in small groups and one large garrison near a mighty power station that we pass.

Our transit visas do not permit us to leave the Autobahn. Well out of the restricted zone where only the direst emergency would justify a stop we pull off the road into a dusty curved lane that serves as a rest area. Within minutes, several other West German vehicles do likewise, as if our example, eight people holding a relaxed coffee break around a vehicle with western license plates, lent others a sense of security.

Hans, ever alert to required formalities, uses the time to fill out currency declarations for each family unit in our party. There is no restriction on the amount of money we can carry with us as long as on our return trip our funds are either diminished or no greater than the sums we take into Poland with us. Before we proceed to the Berlin Ring we refuel, paying a third less per liter of gasoline than in West Germany. Of course, payment is made in western currency—D-marks are desirable.

For reasons that elude me we pass through an uneventful control into West Berlin territory and immediately circle out again to another checkpoint leading back into the German Democratic Republic. Is it my imagination, perhaps a momentary relief at traveling beyond the reach of East Bloc authorities? It seems that I had a fleeting glimpse, like a memory, of tree-lined, wide streets interspersed with neatly trimmed hedges and flowers. After half an hour of waiting, face control, questions and documentation for which Hans is well prepared, we depart once again between barbed-wire fences into an area where fewer western vehicles venture; indeed, there seems to be altogether much less movement on this road than on the western approach to Berlin.

The land is flat. The road, arrow-straight, leads through a few more collectives and then on and on through Prussia's sandbox of the Mark Brandenburg, with its forests of wind-tossed pines whose trunks glow rusty-red in the afternoon sun, and with occasional clusters of birches on sandy knolls. The monotony of the land and the steady hum of the motor lull me to sleep.

Hans's voice cuts through the silence—only then do I realize that we are standing still.

"Rise and shine! Chow is on! You wouldn't be too tired to roll out and eat, would you?"

Our belated picnic lunch is a stand-up meal in a bare, dusty parking place from where a side road runs toward a nearby village. We cannot observe any life between the neat gray rows of houses. Again I am struck by the absence of color, and I miss the vibrant touches of flowers in bloom that enliven every community I have seen in West Germany. Motorcyclists, a couple with a little boy, have stopped near us;

10

without looking at their license plates I can assume them to be natives because their clothing, too, lacks color and frills. Our bright vehicle and bright clothes elicit curious stares, and I cannot help wondering if these might not also be invited by the smell of hot, strong coffee and the richly spread buns, fruit, and cake that we consume greedily in great quantities.

Rolf takes the wheel, and whether from concern for his less experienced driving or because I feel refreshed or because I am getting excited at approaching more familiar territory, I remain awake and alert through all of the monotonous kilometers to the last border we must cross.

By 4:00 P.M. we pull into the checkpoint near Forst where Hans has promised the delight of visiting the duty-free shop at our leisure because he is sure that we can reach our destination easily by 7:00 P.M. I am no longer apprehensive of the border; the formalities seem a mere nuisance and delay. I no longer worry about any careless remark or grimace by my exuberant fifteen-year-old son; he has been exemplarily subdued in our encounters with border guards, except for a moment of general hilarity when one of them glanced through our crowd in search of the alleged two children in our party who, though under sixteen and officially classified as children, look grown-up and are as tall as any of the adults, in fact, even taller. Tom turns his face dutifully straight toward the guard at face control, raises a hand or nods acknowledgment when his name is called; yes, he has taken to heart all the preliminary admonitions to keep his nimble tongue in check and to do exactly as he is told.

We are motioned forward to the last booth to await the return of our passports and are asked to step out of the van. A lean, good-looking officer greets Hans with the usual questions as to where from and where to and the litany of contraband while he leans into the vehicle.

"Let's see what is in this box."

Hans obediently pulls it from under the middle seat and opens the cover:

"A case of wine for the pastor we are going to visit."

"Wine for the pastor? Then I suppose it is blessed. Are you a pastor, too?" the officer asks with a smirk.

Hans can't suppress a wink at his snickering sons before answering in the negative.

What next catches the attention of the officer makes my blood run cold. My note pad, empty except for the first page, lies face down on the back seat. He reaches for it, starts reading.

"What have we here? Well, well, very detailed—date, times, weather, even seating—"

In a light voice that belies my uneasiness I start to explain: "Some notes for later to keep the memory of this—"

When he cuts me off, his voice is anything but light: "Barbed wire? You have seen no barbed wire!"

Helga who starts to speak up in my defense is silenced by a withering look from her husband.

"Such lies," the officer hisses under his breath as he tucks the offensive pad under his arm and focuses on a travel bag with flashlights, batteries, and tools. He takes the bag and asks Hans to follow him into the booth. I look at Hans helplessly and lower my lids before his expression of reproach, resignation, and reassurance. I should have known better, I of all people who worried about my son's understandable lack of caution, I who had experienced East Bloc regimentation once before in my life!

I walk the few steps to a bench beyond the booth and sit down to overcome a sudden weakness. Unobtrusively I can keep the two men in my field of vision. The officer rummages through the bag while they are exchanging talk. Such a small harmless bag and so much talk!

As I join the boys and women who are huddled beside the van I catch the end of Helene's harangue:

"What business of his is it anyway?" and I know what she is so upset about.

Werner whispers beseechingly: "Grandma, they can hear you."

12

"Let them hear the truth," she spits back. "Can't I say what I think?"

Werner counters with another question: "Do you want us to get away from here?"

At that the old woman, red fury-spots on her cheeks, climbs into the van and sits stony-faced in her anger without saying another word.

I resume my pacing, sitting, pacing, then force myself to sit on the bench. At last I see the officer emerge from one door of the booth and Hans from the other, coming straight toward me. My agitation must have been written on my face because his first words in a level voice are:

"Just be calm. I told him that you don't understand the situation here and may have read something in America that put ideas in your head. But, for heaven's sake, have you forgotten your English? Did you have to write in German?"

I lamely try to justify how the recent weeks in West Germany make it more natural to write in German about German affairs.

"Write all you want but from now on in English. Few, if any of these clowns, will be able to read it then and won't want to admit it. And one more thing: If any of them should talk to you, say amen or whatever they want to hear!"

His timely advice is put to the test shortly. Our nemesis approaches with my note pad in his hand.

"So you are the scribbler," he greets me sarcastically.

Hans is at my side, making me feel less afraid.

"You are a typical victim of enemy propaganda. You believe every lie you hear or read and then think you see what they have told you. You don't really believe that we have barbed wire on our border, or need it, do you?"

The handsome face recedes and there are only pale-green, sharp eyes glaring at me. While I hesitate, Hans reiterates his apologia to spare me the answer, but he is rudely interrupted by the officer:

"Here you come along one road through our country and think you know everything. What do you really know?

Nothing! Sure, you saw collectives—did you also see the work that goes on there and everywhere? We have built our nation by hard work from scratch without anyone's help, and we are strong and proud of our socialist state. If you want to see barbed wire, look at rolls and rolls of it on the Berlin Wall—yes, it is there. And do you know why? Not to keep our people in but to keep out the meddlers who won't leave us alone. You just think you saw it elsewhere, and you write it down as fact, and then you will talk about it when you get home, perhaps even publish such rubbish! People like you spread lies about us, and others gladly believe them because that is what they want to hear. If you really want to see progress and experience how we live, spend a vacation in our country instead of forming a snap judgment of lies in passing through—"

Won't he ever stop? I have been an American too long to tolerate the heated monologue without a sense of outrage and the urge to contradict him. Worst of all are the piercing "Do you understand?" and "Don't you see?" that punctuate his relentless socialist lecture and to which I have been ordered to respond positively, albeit as noncommittally as I can contrive to answer. To keep what I would like to say from showing in my eyes I let them wander intermittently, and then back to the face of my mentor whom I can picture in other uniforms at other times, and in whatever disguise each picture signals "fanatic"—"incurable"—"dangerous"—"desperate." There is no softness anywhere in the young, well-structured face, none in the finely chiseled nose or the narrow lips, nor in the eyes that are as hard and cold as a steel blade. The lecture runs its course, and I make my obligatory responses in monosyllables, until he has done his patriotic duty and curtly hands the note pad back to me. And that is more than I had expected. I am too dazed to say anything to the others in the van, but Hans diagnoses the case promptly as he pulls into the parking area on the Polish side:

"I knew this character's mind was set on provocation when he first opened his mouth to needle me about the wine.

Once in a while you run up against a 150-percent radical, and then you must play it very cool."

One of them ever is enough for me, I think to myself, as I fluctuate between cold fury and hot waves of humiliation.

"Let's get out of here and forget about the duty-free shop," I plead.

"Quit worrying—he is through with us. Besides, here is the currency exchange—"

While he trades our money coupons, which we had to buy before visas to Poland were issued, we look at the merchandise, mainly alcoholic beverages, cigarettes, candy—all of Polish, British, and American brands—and lose ourselves in admiration before a showcase with hand-cut lead crystal. All prices are marked in dollars, but any western currency is acceptable. Except for a supply of good, inexpensive Polish vodka with a long blade of grass floating in the bottle and some cigarettes for anticipated bribes, Hans urges us to leave any shopping for the return trip. I am still too uneasy and angry anyhow to enjoy it and cannot relax until the border lies far behind us.

What a pity that the episode at the very last checkpoint we have to pass overshadows the memory of the polite and pleasant border guards up to that time. Ironically, the man who chided me for distorting with lies the picture of his country was the one to confirm how true they are. The price for my lesson in socialism was two hours of daylight lost and the exposure to those cold, cold eyes that continue to haunt me.

Through the soft light of the summer evening the road we travel now takes us in a southeasterly direction. I experience the first unnerving touch of disorientation because the road signs are in Polish in this area where the name of every town ought to have a familiar ring. Hans hands a map back to me, and by remembered location and direction I begin to identify our route through the western part of Silesia.

After we leave the Autobahn we pass through small communities that mean nothing to me, neither by their Polish nor their former German name, and merely stir a sad feeling because of the denuded look of old houses that are uncared for, interspersed with a few raw, new buildings, functional and square, lacking beauty. When the early fog steams up from the meadows at dusk, the road begins to wind and rise and fall with the gentle slopes. Now I desperately want to see because I know that we are approaching the mountains that are home. I can barely discern them on the darkening horizon when night shrouds them, returning them to the world of memory yet again.

More than thirty years ago I had passed this way in the opposite direction under military guard toward an undisclosed destination. Behind me lay a childhood, secure in love and promises, and youth devastated by a lost war; ahead gaped a void bleaker than that encountered by a newborn child because there was no one to count on for the very necessities of life, no resources but the bags against which I leaned in the shuddering freight car. This journey into uncertainty did not end for me until I had staked claim to a life in a new country, far removed in miles and mind from a past that I did not want to remember and, in the end, could not forget.

Old diaries, written in a script that no child learns to write any more, penned in fading ink on wartime paper, lay buried for many years before I had the courage to open them, and when I did, memories took possession of me with a force and vividity undiminished by the passage of time and became more real than the events of recent weeks. Homesickness with an almost masochistic streak lured me into planning this trip "home," which I knew existed no more. Afraid of losing again what I had lost before, I began to record the visions and voices from the past to keep them undistorted by the scenes I am about to see thirty years later.

Tomorrow is still far away. Behind the mountains in this summer night lies the home of my memories.

1

Childhood Scenes

Villa Fürstenhof

Dreams of childhood are enclosed by a high wrought-iron fence, perhaps not so high for a father who could look over it, but very high for a little girl who might stretch to reach the tips and then settle for a lower peek between the bars.

The gate to the sidewalk at the end of a long paved path was always closed and so were other gates toward the quiet street in back and toward the expanse of lawn where the women bleached their linens on sunny days. The house was set well back from the street in the center of hedges and paths that led to a gazebo or lost themselves in the bushes. Wide steps rose to a stone terrace at its front, and on several levels the delicate grillwork of balconies protruded and even jutted out from the corner turrets. On the opposite side of the street, single family homes in small well-tended gardens were crowded, without gentle transition, by a stark new housing development of small duplexes, which bordered on the sidewalk without a hedge or strip of grass to grace their nakedness. A world apart, devoid of charm, and worlds away from the big house in the parklike garden.

Once the big house had been a resort hotel, and smaller

buildings behind it had housed the staff and the carriages for the use of the guests. A mountain of coal and tools of all kinds now filled the low carriage house, and only the family of the caretaker occupied the two-story staff house. The big house had become the property of the government and had been converted into large apartments for a dozen or so fortunate civil servants who worked in the city about fifteen streetcar minutes away from the small health resort.

For the children of our family, who lived there, Villa Fürstenhof, guarded by the high spiked fence and the cloak of greenery, was our whole world. In the winter the sloping lawn of the drying patch became our first course for sledding and skiing, and in summer the bushes and trees came alive with our giggles and shrieks in games of hide-and-seek. The enchanting place regressed to past glory at birthday time, and lucky the child whose birthday happened on a balmy summer day! Then a table with sweets and coffee might be set in the rectangular garden house near the fence or in a smaller gazebo in the center of the park.

It may have been my third or fourth birthday which I remember so well, or perhaps another year when a special friend was not allowed to come out of her parents' respect for President von Hindenburg who had died on the day of the celebration. No matter—all summer birthdays followed the same general format and in memory merge into one party, full of charm and fun.

They began in the early afternoon after the civil servants had finished their noonday rest and returned to their offices in the city. The children hurried through the festive ritual of birthday coffee and cake to run into the garden for games of blind man's bluff and races and an endless variety of ball games. Quieter games followed, with prizes for the best riddle solver, the tallest or smallest or youngest or oldest—everybody was a winner of some sort. Our housekeeper and nurse, Heia, who was the genius of the party, saw to everyone's fun and never forgot to make the birthday child feel the star.

For supper we gathered inside for hot sausages and cold

potato salad, and we enlivened the meal with our favorite game of stop-and-go while we munched away. The child who was "it" had the power to freeze everybody else in the middle of a bite or swallow with the shout "*Halt!*" producing giggles of delight at the open mouths and suspended forks and almost tipped glasses of the statues at the table, until a call of "*Weiter!*" released them to laughter and a few uninterrupted mouthfuls.

Meanwhile the preparations for the grande finale of the best day of the year proceeded under the cloak of gathering dusk. As we filed downstairs into the garden, each child was handed a Japanese lantern and exhorted to hold it tightly and steadily to keep the candle inside burning brightly and the lantern safe. Flanked by the glow of colorful lanterns, I passed through the lines of guests to settle in my place of honor in a wooden handcart garlanded with the flowers of the season. Heia, as she pulled the cart, tuned up a song and all chimed in, and the procession floated through the grounds in the swaying light of the lanterns to the sound of happy voices.

Parents or older brothers and sisters came to claim the little guests. The gate clanked shut after the last of them, and silence and darkness settled on the small paradise inside the spiked wrought-iron fence that held the dreams of childhood.

Christmas

Christmas began on the day when Mama melted the butter and honey in an enormous tin pan and asked Father, who never entered the kitchen except to look into the pots on the stove, to work the heavy dough after she had added the flour and her arms had grown weary from stirring and kneading. For a day the fragrance of spices permeated the house and was then confined to crocks and boxes in secret places. Christmas went underground for several weeks after that, but a lingering sense of anticipation remained hovering about.

Christmas Eve seemed subdued and drab, yet busy, and no one had time for us children. Father locked himself in the dining room, and afterwards locked the door from the outside. The noon meal was light and hurried, allowing for the fast the grownups observed and for the cleaning which disrupted playtime, naptime and any good time for us as long as daylight lasted. The early dusk of the winter evening, when normally the lights would have been turned on, brought the family together for a recitation of the rosary, with Father leading the prayers and never cheating by so much as one Ave Maria. The long chain of repetitive prayers, even though the "joyous" secrets were being recited, seemed interminable to us children. We suppressed a sigh of relief after the last Pater Noster, which signaled the end of the dark and the approach of the long-awaited festivities.

The traditional fare of Christmas Eve supper consisted of roasted veal sausages, sauerkraut, and mashed potatoes. After eating the meal in the kitchen, we were condemned to a restless waiting period, while Mama and Heia cleared the table and washed dishes, and then changed from their house dresses into more festive clothes. Father once more secluded himself in the dining room while we children stood in the hallway, taking turns at a peek through the keyhole. At last Mama and Heia joined us, admonishing us to be sweet and still.

The magic moment was at hand. A tiny bell tinkled behind the locked door. Father opened it, revealing a room transformed by the gently flickering candles on the tall tree on which glistening stars and other baubles, gilded nuts and polished apples, colored sweets and decorated ginger cookies shone gaily. On the buffet the manger with the Holy Family was surrounded by shepherds and their flock, and angels floated above on strings from the ceiling. The dining table was set for the whole family, with presents laid in each place instead of dishes, with bowls of nuts, fruit, and cookies in the center. Just inside the door, impatiently jostling, we came to a halt and lined up for caroling. As we grew older, those of us who had learned to play an instrument accompanied the songs on the piano, violin, and recorder. This last test of our patience was as unchanging as the rosary in the deepening shadows of the afternoon had been.

During the carols we had already spotted our presents, which were lined and stacked on the table without wrappings, and at last we were allowed to rush over to them. Never elaborate or excessive, the gifts were mostly pieces of clothing just a step beyond the strictly functional or necessary, games for all to share, craft projects, and books to the taste of each child or some of new interest if our parents had detected a slumbering talent or budding concern. Father never failed to get a flask of rum to lace his tea on cold winter evenings, while Mama and Heia feigned surprise and delight at small accessories and materials for needlework or a laboriously finished piece of stitchery from one of us girls.

When the presents had been examined and admired, perhaps tried on or put together, they were set aside to make room on the table for an evening of games for the whole family. Father brewed hot spiced wine that glowed deep-red in the crystal glasses, while cheeks all around began to glow as well and eyes to sparkle with pleasure.

Christmas Eve always kept its promise of warmth and love and happiness. As long as Father was there to preside over tradition and ritual, it never lost all of its magic, even after Mama died and Heia had been sent away, and after we children became old enough to face the terrifying reality of our secure world foundering.

All who could stave off sleep bundled up to brave the winter night for midnight mass. In snowy seasons the old town looked like a picture on a Christmas card. Street lamps were bathed in a halo of golden light in the still, icy air, and each post and protrusion wore a furry cap, as the isolated churchgoers crunched their way over the frozen pavement.

The shepherd's mass in the cathedrallike church was a tender, intimate adoration of the Child in the manger. As the lights suddenly flooded the nave with their brilliance, the choir burst into glorious chants backed by the roaring and lilting of organ and cymbals and violins and the roll of the drum. The cold stone building pulsed with the vibrant, jubilant celebration of God in the highest, and the lofty pillars drew the hearts of those who heard and saw upward and beyond all earthly cares. Such was the power and beauty of the service that it attracted believers and unbelievers alike to impart to all the joyful tidings of Christmas.

Nothing in the days that followed could compete with the riches of Christmas Eve, not the roast-goose dinner on Christmas Day, nor the fortune-telling fun on New Year's Eve. When the statues of the Three Wise Men were added to the manger scene on their feast day, January 6, the candles on the tree were lighted one last time, while we children searched its tired branches for forgotten nuts and candy decorations, before it was stripped of all its finery. Christmas was over once again, leaving in its wake the memories of shared love in the name of a little child and promising ever to return to rekindle faith and hope and love until all men would heed its message of peace.

Sunday

On a gloomy Sunday morning in November, when a light drizzle moistened the deserted sidewalks in the old part of town, two boys and two girls left home for the late children's mass. Paired in our usual fashion, with the younger boy—Gerhard—and the littlest girl—Annemarie (Annemie for short)—in front barely restraining their high spirits, and the slightly older pair—Franz and I—following more sedately, arms linked, we walked around the square where colonnades along the storefronts shielded us from the raw morning air. A short block beyond the square, past the picket fence of the convent, we crossed a cobblestoned plaza surrounding the red-brick church whose Gothic spires reached toward the sky. In the church we took our accustomed seats in the family pew, knelt, and sang the familiar hymns as on many other Sundays strung together like the beads of a rosary.

Yet, this was not a Sunday morning like any other, and we felt it more than we knew and were troubled by it in the way that any child is disturbed by an unusual break in the routine of the parental household. While Heia's kindly hands had straightened the caps and secured the buttons on our Sunday coats, the family doctor had come to call to look in on Mama, who had not shared breakfast with us and who had gone to bed early because of a headache on the previous evening. Mama had had headaches before—why bother the doctor with such a small matter, especially on Sunday morning? With change in our pockets to put into the collection basket for the poor and for masses to be said for the poor souls in purgatory, we had set out on our walk to church as usual.

Mass was almost over and all knelt to respond to the closing prayers, which the priest offered for the special concerns of the parishioners. As he intoned the last Ave Maria for a dying mother, the death bell that is more a whimper than a ringing began to speak its mournful message.

After the inhibiting decorum of the church service we stepped quickly through the light rain, taking the shortest course home to a hot dinner and an afternoon of games and books near the radiant tile stove. The door was opened to us into a very still hallway. No sound of Father's favorite program of classical music and no fragrance of spicy soup and pot roast and sweet-sour cabbage wafted toward us on that day.

The bell had tolled for Mama. She had died without awakening, as quietly as she had lived, on this gloomy, drizzly Sunday morning in November.

Heia

She was barely five feet tall, and as children we thought that her small size had something to do with the fact that she was a twin. She seemed to have never been young because even in our earliest memories her hair, which was fastened tightly in a bun on top of her head, was streaked with gray.

Mama had engaged her as nurse and housekeeper when the first child was born to share with her the responsibility for running the household to suit Father's expectations and to rear the children. Except for Mama's ever growing reliance on her and the confidences born of their daily closeness, Heia remained outside the family, took her meals alone in the kitchen, worked there deep into the night ironing and mending the family linen and wardrobe, before retiring to her austere little room. She rarely left the house for her own pleasure, except to go to church, to meetings of a group of pious spinsters, or to visit her equally tiny twin sister.

Father's formal relationship to her, however, which never softened throughout her years of service, could not keep us children from attaching ourselves to her, beginning with our first faltering steps. She became our mentor, the voice that admonished and praised, the last resort for begging special favors, and the hand that soothed and comforted. Being small almost like us, we made her our playmate and sometimes, in childish willfulness, the one to bear our irritation and anger. Father viewed her importance to us with some disapproval, but Mama never showed any resentment but rather relief that she herself was spared the constant care or demands of the children. Perhaps following a premonition, Mama seemed to withdraw gradually from our activities and to entrust more and more supervision to her much more energetic and patient alter ego.

The two women, so different in personality and background and social station, merged into one mother who, combined, lavished on us more love and guidance than either one alone would have had the physical and spiritual capacity to give. Mama's were the quiet hours when she taught us girls the arts of needlecraft in which she excelled, and when she reminisced about her serene childhood on the big farm with a hierarchy of servants who secretly practiced superstitious rites to make the animals and fields fruitful, or when she told of her years in the convent where she was sent to learn the demeanor and skills of a well-bred young lady. Hers also was the joy of making frilly new dresses for us out of little more than her imagination and skill, to plait our long dark hair and fasten bows in it, or to go on long family walks, with Father strutting proudly ahead between his daughters and Mama following in her Sunday best between the two sons she adored. Mama reigned in the kitchen, planning and putting her own touch on the meals for which Heia had done the marketing and initial preparations. The delicacies for family feasts and for birthday parties came from Mama's hands, but on these latter occasions she left the fun and games with us to Heia and enjoyed them from a distance.

Together they loved and labored for their family. Heia thought of us children as her own as much and with as much right as Mama did. She called us her "golden angels" and by other effusive endearments and, at other times, preached to us with the fervor of an outraged guardian of law and order. What she lacked in parental authority, which we would not have dared question, she made up for by cajoling and spoiling us and by sheer tenacity laced with tenderness.

Heia kept life going in its accustomed way when Mama died. Father conceded that she should serve and eat at the family table and handle the household allowance under his watchful eye. She kept the memory of Mama alive and invoked her name when one of us made her dual role difficult. Much later she told of her promise to Mama to watch over us as long as we needed her. She never broke that promise, even after a new maid took Heia's place in our house.

In the second year after Mama's death Father remarried. Accustomed as he was to our obedience and general harmony with his decisions, he assumed that we would accept his new wife as our mother and address her as such. This formality became an obstacle, especially for me, his favorite. "Number Two," as I called her to myself, was a presence to be ignored more than politely possible, but eventually even I had to force myself to call her Mother for lack of an acceptable alternative, yet not without the bite of resentment in the sound of it.

As long as Heia was still with us, our life-long attachment to her made Mother an outsider rather than the mistress of the house. This living reminder of Mama became intolerable to both Father and Mother and had to go. When Heia left, we lost our Mama a second time, but in our hearts her place was secure and untouchable.

Father insisted on a complete break from the old servant, and to save his face, we never defied him openly. But friends and relatives conspired to arrange clandestine meetings so that Heia could see the children who were her life. After several unhappy years in distant positions, she contrived to find work in the city where we then lived. By then teenagers, we paid her frequent visits in secret, sometimes merely in search of tenderness, sometimes for the treats she kept ready for us at a time when food itself had become a treat. It took a tragedy to reveal that Father knew where she was and that he knew of our disobedience to him and our loyalty to our most loyal friend.

Glatz

The rhythmic clatter of soldiers' boots on the pavement was a familiar sound in the garrison town. A regiment had been based permanently in the barracks at the edge of town as long as anyone could remember, except for the interval between the two World Wars, when the Treaty of Versailles severely limited Germany's military forces.

The garrison cemetery on a rise not far from the business district bore silent testimony to centuries of wars that had swept over the area. There in the shade of ancient trees lay the dead soldiers, friend and foe side by side, peaceful at last in eternal sleep. Many of the graves were still well-tended by generations surviving the dead; in others, uncared for, lay the remains of men long forgotten, their rain- and wind-beaten markers revealing only an occasional date or a foreign sign as a clue to the identity of their occupants. A metal half-moon was rusting on the grave of a dead Turk whose life had ended here far from home centuries ago. In the ebb and flow of political wrangles the territory had been part of the Kingdom of Bohemia and of the Austro-Hungarian Empire and later had come under Prussian rule, long after it had been overrun by Huns and Slavs and the most advanced forces of the Ottoman Empire.

Perched on a steep promontory, the fortress dominated the panorama. The houses of the oldest part of town, huddled against the base of the fortress, and the narrow cobble-stoned streets seemed forever darkened by the shadow of the mighty bulwark. Even the square from which the city hall rose in time-worn splendor conveyed the impression of a town in danger, perhaps under siege; here the well of Saint Mary, now within a weathered wrought-iron enclosure, provided water for the townspeople and the protection of their patron saint in times of extremity.

The small city was located at the entrance to a gently rising and falling valley that was surrounded by a rectangle of mountain ranges on all sides. Few streets ran level and straight for more than a block but conformed to the natural contours of the land. All roads and railways from the plain of Silesia converged on the town through the only opening in the rectangle of mountains. From the city they fanned out in southerly and westerly directions into a land of serene beauty, interspersed with small streams and wooded hills that were dwarfed by the ever-present view of the bordering ranges, some of which harbored snow from one winter to the next in hidden crevices. From the highest range rose the tallest peak in the area, the *Schneeberg* ("Snow Mountain"), which was visible throughout the valley on a clear day. When the snow on the surrounding slopes melted in the spring, the gurgling brooks turned into devastating torrents, swelling the larger streams that flowed into the Neisse River, and wreaking disasters in the small towns and villages on the banks. When the waters receded and their traces had been removed, the people returned to their peaceful pursuits of farming humble fields that climbed high on the slopes and of tending their crafts.

Hardly any industry soiled the air in this land which seemed sealed off by nature from the wealth and haste of the plain to the east. While progress seemed to have passed it by, this secluded area was destined to become a haven for vacationers who in winter flocked from the cities outside to the mountain lodges for winter sport. Even far more in summer the visitors came, some for a day and some for weeks, to enjoy the clean air and the countless opportunities for excursions in the wooded hills and craggy mountains. The ranges protected the land from the violent weather of the plain and often seemed to tame it dramatically before it transgressed beyond them. Conversely, once caught among the peaks, the clouds seemed to remain imprisoned until they had spent themselves.

Scattered throughout the uneven valley and invading the seclusion of the dark woods, resorts beckoned the ill to seek renewed health at their healing wells and baths. The reputation of these spas spread far and wide and retains its attraction even in the present medicine-oriented age. The local people also enjoyed the beauty and small-scale elegance of these resorts and joined the visitors on leisurely days, strolling through the halls where healing waters spouted from ornate wells into marble basins, walking on flower-edged paths through the parks, and relaxing on shaded benches to the strains of the resort orchestra. None of the spas was too distant to visit on a Sunday afternoon and return by evening on one of the frequent trains that traversed the area, stopping briefly at each village en route.

Once Austria had been annexed and Czechoslovakia usurped to form Greater Germany in the late thirties, the express trains from Berlin to Vienna on their roundabout way through Silesia passed through Glatz for a stop between the provincial capital and Prague. Still in the future are other trains that will herald a change on the political horizon. From the beginning of World War II seemingly endless troop trains will roll through the narrow mountain passes between east and west, freight cars from which soldiers on a short pause will reach for the proffered cups of coffee and sandwiches from the hands of women volunteers. Almost incessantly, open flatcars will carry the murderous weapons of modern warfare to the Eastern Front from the industrial centers of the south and west, and local passenger trains will be shunted on a side rail for these ominous loads.

Then the historical city once again takes on a military character but unlike any it had known in the past. Through the original barracks, which had been the home of one provincial regiment, passes a constantly changing procession of young recruits who speak in the dialects of distant parts of Germany and for whom this remote mountain country seems almost foreign because they had never heard of it. They cannot know that now they walk on German soil that will remain unscarred and safe far longer than any other to the very last day of the war.

On one of the hills into which new residential districts extend toward the woods, an Army Communications Center is based in row upon row of new permanent buildings. Through it flows a stream of soldiers for short-term technical courses. For the fortunate members of the *Luftwaffe* who have survived a clash with the enemy, a huge camp of low-slung cottages has sprung up as a rest home in the seclusion of the ascending woods. Buildings in and around town, schools and the homes of religious orders, become hospitals seemingly overnight to receive the wounded who are fit to be transported and to be restored through convalescence for return to danger and death.

The town is teeming with men in uniform who live a temporary respite from the grim reality they will all have to face in days or months or years to come. Their rousing songs rise above the marching tread over the cobblestoned streets and make the townspeople step sprightly in unison with them. The evidence of the wounds others have suffered spurs the people to an ever greater willingness to sacrifice in their own lives and to bear the privations imposed upon them without rancor, even with gratitude for being safe and well and able to welcome these strangers into their relative peace.

For almost six years they are confident that woods and mountains and the blessings of the Virgin will shield the area from the ravages of air attacks and invasion.

Glatz of World War II days is the town I remember as my home.

2
War Years: 1939–1944

⟋⟍

School Days

After summer vacation of 1939, I return to the building in which I spent the last school year, and yet it is a different school. Of the former faculty, only a few lay teachers will continue teaching; all of the nuns who had been teachers and administrators are gone.

For me, this change means a return to the kind of inter-denominational girls' school which I had attended in another town before Father's promotion and the family's move to Glatz. Here, given the choice between two private schools—one Protestant, the other a Catholic boarding school—I was enrolled as a day student in the convent school. Bordering on the school grounds was the attractive dormitory for the boarders; behind it, separated by a large garden, stood the orphanage. The community of nuns had taken care of all of these enterprises and had enjoyed the respect of the area people for providing an excellent institution of learning.

With a guilty feeling of relief, I reflect on the departure of the nuns. I had been motivated mainly by fear of the Madame Director to study the conjugation of foreign verbs to perfection and had been resentful of too many devotions at chapel and too many religious allusions throughout the school day. On the other hand, Sister Humilitas had brought history to life for me as no other teacher ever could, presenting ancient events with perspective and human interest, and the spunky Sister Laurentia had made tedious piano practice a challenge and a joy.

But the nuns, whether remembered affectionately or with distaste, are gone now because their presence and prominence are incompatible with the Nazi regime. They have been discredited and disowned. The dormitory has become the residence of a high party official, and the school has been secularized and expanded to include the orphanage building. The few nuns remaining in town have found shelter in the attic apartment of a local pharmacist whose large house is located opposite their former property, and there they eke out an existence with private tutoring and secret alms. Where have the others gone? Where are the orphans for whom they cared? Even a child cannot accept without question or qualm what has happened without apparent justice or explanation.

The crucifix on the wall of each classroom has been replaced by a portrait of the *Führer*, and at the beginning of each class we stand at attention to greet our new teachers with raised right arms. No doubt remains in whose spirit the new administration will conduct the school.

Hardly settled into the routines of the school year 1939–40 in our new school, we are caught up in a different kind of excitement. Germany is at war! The early fall days ring with the rousing news of battles won. In celebration of the victories, classes are often dismissed early, that being an additional cause for rejoicing. The victories, first in Poland and later in the Lowlands and France, become so commonplace that soon they are only mentioned and cheered in class without the bonus time-off.

War is still a great adventure when our classes of girls in their teens assemble in rugged clothing for a day of rural service. We march through the spring morning shouldering picks and hoes, cheered by the prospect of a day out of school, to spend long hours weeding the fields on a large farm not far from town. Supervised by a teacher, we hack at the thistles and clean the furrows as well as we know how. Somewhat less pleasant are damp and chilly days in the fall when we have to help farmers in the potato harvest.

Coal grows scarcer every winter. While our school remains unheated and closed during weeks of the most severe cold, our classes are scheduled in alternating shifts with those at the vocational school. It seems like an extended Christmas vacation to have some unusual hours free for skiing and ice-skating. Outdoor clothing and heavy boots become accepted outfits to be worn to school because even the heated classrooms at the vocational school are far from warm. Yet, with typical youthful shortsightedness, we enjoy these hardship measures because they disrupt the drab routine of the school year.

During one summer vacation the older girls have a choice between volunteering for *Unternehmen Barthold*—a project of digging trenches behind the Eastern Front—to care for the boys of the Hitler Youth who labored there or of remaining at home to work and harvest in the garden plot behind the school and then to can fruits and vegetables for use of the army hospitals in town. By what criteria did I happen to become a gardener and canner, contrary to any natural inclination? Perhaps by disinclination to volunteer for anything or by virtue of having been appointed group leader of a *Jung-mädel* unit in a nearby rural community. While the assignment a few blocks from home pleases my parents, I experience qualms at times that my place should be in the thick of things directly related to events at the front.

As months grow into years, war intrudes more and more into the life of each of us. For many girls, fathers and older brothers are reduced to letters from faraway places, often unnamed for security reasons, across the reaches of Europe and Africa and the seas. No matter how brief or insignificant, each letter carries the all-important message "Alive!"

More frequent become the letters from home that are returned unopened and marked *Empfänger gefallen für Gross-deutschland*, and more frequent the black arm bands that signify mourning, but instead of the customary months, people now wear these briefly because they are frowned upon officially. Death for the fatherland is to be thought an honor rather than a loss and cause for grief.

Two of my friends have lost their only brothers on the Eastern Front. We all suffer with them because there are few who cannot identify with them. Thank God, my brother Franz is still in occupied France and in no immediate danger, and Gerhard still a few months away from induction. Yet, his turn is bound to come because the prospects of ending the war, instead of improving, seem to be moving farther away.

One Sunday morning in June, I return from church and find Mother in tears and Father looking grim.

"That's the end for all of us," she mumbles between sobs.

"What is?" I ask, assuming a domestic crisis of unusual proportions.

"Our troops have marched into Russia," states Father with an almost solemn air that transmits to me, more than Mother's tears, the gravity of this new development.

A few months later we are stunned by Japan's attack on America, but no one is surprised that as Japan's ally we, too, are at war with America now. Our soldiers already stand in every country in Europe. How can they wage war against another continent separated by an ocean? Mother doesn't cry any more, but often while she sits sewing her lips move in silent prayer.

During one Christmas vacation we get our first inkling of what people in the northern and western cities have experienced for months. I don't know which awakened me, the shrill door bell or someone shouting "Alarm!" into my room or the wailing siren, all happening simultaneously. Within moments, Father herds the whole family, attired in whatever was at hand topped with warm coats, into the *Heldenkeller*, ("hero cellar"), as the hallway of the basement is dubbed. Our maid is shaking with fright and whimpering. Once the penetrating howl of the siren has faded away, everyone feels calmer. We listen for planes and detonations. But the next

34

sound we hear outside is the long drawn-out *Entwarnung* ("all clear"). After half an hour in the chilly basement we return shivering to our now cold beds. Sleep does not come immediately. Instead I practice mentally the first-aid procedures that I have learned in recent meetings of the *Bund deutscher Mädchen* ("German Girls League"), including how to approach victims through burning and smoke-filled rooms, and I imagine every nook and cranny of our half-block-long basement shelter in ghastly conflagration. How seemingly real one alarm can make situations we had just practiced.

Most of the time after school is now devoted to activities directly related to the war, but not all of them unpleasant or serious. In groups from school or from the *BDM*, we sing for the wounded in one or another of the many hospitals around town. Father on his own also goes to visit the wounded and when asked for books or minor personal items lets Annemie or me deliver these later.

But such visits to relatively lightly wounded have not prepared me for an amputee ward through which a health-training group of *BDM*-girls is shown for instructional purposes. Suffering and mutilations all around us, I find myself standing next to an elderly couple at the foot of one of the beds. In it lies what is left of a very young man, his face suffused with a translucent pallor and his head attached to what appears to be a rectangular package under the sheets. In a matter-of-fact voice, the group leader introduces to us the first quadruple amputee we have seen, expounding to us and his parents on the capabilities of military medicine. Revolted by her callousness as much as by the sight of the barely living wreckage, I must turn away with an inexplicable sense of shame and guilt. The picture of the dying young soldier remains before me, superimposed on the glorious face of war and distorting it into a terrifying grimace.

All we at home can do to make our distant soldiers' lot easier is to write to them, and we wield the pen with fervor. Writing to every family member in uniform is only the beginning, and expected. At the other extreme we become pen pals out of patriotic duty with soldiers we don't know and may never meet. A classmate's father who commands a division in Russia sends to his daughter the names of soldiers who seldom receive mail. Of course, we will write to them! No matter how trivial the accounts of teenage larks and frustrations, these distant men will then believe that home is still intact and fairly normal and that they are not forgotten. My friend Erika is the first to hear from her unknown soldier, and we laugh and cry together because he speaks of his loneliness and how much it means to know of her sympathetic heart back home. In due course, I hear from the soldier whose name I had drawn. But this frontline correspondence as so many is cut short by bullets.

In between the letters to family and strangers are those to childhood friends who have grown up to be soldiers, brothers' friends who suddenly remember previously ignored little sisters, to flirtatious lieutenants from the hospital once again on active duty, to chance acquaintances from train trips. Be they lonely, bored, frightened, or unhappy, or in search of a little diversion or even love on paper, our world seems full of men eager for our letters.

And how precious theirs are to us! I conspire with our maid to hide all *Feldpost* addressed to me under my pillow before Father has a chance to scrutinize it. In return, I confide to her the most delicious phrases from some of the letters. Once by chance, Father picks up a letter to me off the floor below the mail slot just as I reach for it, having recognized the handwriting of my current favorite, a paratrooper lieutenant. Shrieking I tear it from his hand and make for the privacy of the bathroom. How he laughs when I emerge with a long face, holding in my hand the old empty envelope which he had retrieved from the waste basket and "mailed" to tease me! But I forgive his prank because he keeps me supplied with good stationery, which is hard to come by.

This total war demands dedication from everyone, young and old, male and female, and we feel like comrades-in-arms with our soldiers when we use our pens to support their weapons.

Most frequently I write to Franz, but lately I falter when

I am full of news about the boys who take me home from dancing lessons and when I want to tell him how I love to whirl over the parquet floor in someone's arms. We are lucky to be allowed the customary dancing lessons as an "educational" pursuit because dancing in public places has now been prohibited as an inappropriate activity in these serious times. When Franz had learned ballroom dancing, he emerged without interest in any particular girl; dancing to him meant graceful movement to music, which he loves, and a concession to the *bon ton*. In these matters I find it easier to take Gerhard into my confidence; while he cares little for music or dancing, he understands the fun and flirtations that go with it. Until now, he rarely acted like a big brother, was always teasing and tormenting me, but now he wants to know what company I keep and to advise me on my choice of dancing partners. From school he knows all of the boys in our crowd, and among the girls he knows the pretty ones and my closest friends. To Franz, five years older than I, most of these are strangers; perhaps that explains why my current preoccupations seem of little interest to him.

Gerhard has become very considerate and even shines my shoes and gives me his socks to darn because I do a better job than Mother's hurried stitching. I will miss him when he has to report to service in the *Reichsarbeitsdienst* ("National Labor Service") and after that to some branch of the military. We have grown closer than we ever were.

Being together with my brothers takes on a new significance for me because we know that it will not last. Soon Gerhard will be going away. When Franz comes home on leave, the best time is when he first arrives, sometimes completely unannounced, and we still have the whole leave ahead of us; when he takes off his uniform and is part of us again. Being together with anyone has this sense of transience about it. The vacations I spend in Breslau with my honorary cousin Marianne, who is Mother's niece and not related to me at all, seem intensified because Breslau has many air raids, not as harmless as ours, or when she visits at our house and we talk and giggle constantly, we seem to overreact.

Having gained Marianne for a "cousin," is for me the best part of Father's second marriage. We met a few years ago, when Father arranged a Sunday outing in one of the resorts with his then fiancée and her sister Gretl, who brought her two daughters to get acquainted with Annemie and me. It was love at first sight for Marianne and me. We were opposites in every way—her pig tails blond and mine almost black; she almost scrawny and I on the chubby side; she bubbling with talk and laughter, and I quiet on the outside, just waiting to be swept along into fun. She now looks and acts the part of a big-city girl, and her sparkling good looks dazzle not only boys but men. I can't keep track of all of her romantic entanglements but the stories of her conquests keep us deliciously entertained. Sometimes I envy her, but playing with love as lightly as she does is not part of my nature.

When Marianne visits, the barometer in our house rises a few points. Father tolerates an inordinate amount of levity from her because she is Mother's favorite niece. Once when Gerhard remarked that Marianne was getting on his nerves, Mother denounced him to Father for this insult to her relative, and storm clouds came rolling in. For me, Marianne is pure sunshine because her overabundance of high spirits draws me out of my reticence. She is always full of plans and races from one activity to the next as if time were running out. Perhaps it is.

Our soldiers are in danger, and we at home are no longer safe. If I did not believe in victory, I would despair. Sometimes now, instead of the celebrated conquests, the best news tells of enemy breakthroughs averted and positions held against overwhelming forces. Names of places remembered from lightning advances of previous years sound like eerie echoes mocking the retreating German armies.

Other news, too, is disturbing. The Catholic girls at school were outraged when recently a popular priest from a neighboring town was arrested and sent to a concentration camp. What could he have said in a sermon to justify such harsh punishment? *Justice* and *right*—these words are stock terms in every political speech we hear. Is there more than one kind of right and justice? And what about the doctor we used to know: On an *Eintopf-Sonntag*, when everyone is obligated to have a simple, one-pot meal and donate the savings for the needy, he accompanied his donation with a careless remark: "Here you come again to collect for prolonging the war." He, too, was arrested.

Father doesn't like it when we talk about such things at home. We eat our one-pot Sunday dinners as required and donate. Father insists that we go to church and listen to sermons, even if it means getting up at dawn for the excursionists' mass to be on time for a youth rally that lasts all morning. Regularly we meet the priest who sponsors our religious instruction in his apartment instead of a public building. We do our duty to our country as we must, and we pray a lot.

Gerhard

On this early spring day, when any excuse would do to get out of the house into the sunshine, I take a leisurely stroll through town. With notebooks purchased at the most distant bookstore under my arm, I am on my way home, walking more briskly now, not for lack of time but because the deceptive sunshine is still powerless against the chill in the air. In the center of town by the hardware store, I enter the private door that leads to the upstairs residence of the owner. Rarely do I come this way without stopping for a brief visit with our old servant, Heia, who now works in the household of the storeowner.

Heia is at home as usual and delighted to see one of us children whom she holds dear as if her own. I sit down at the kitchen table near the coal stove and relax in the warmth it spreads, while Heia busies herself pouring hot coffee and unwrapping a slice of cake left over from the previous Sunday, talking all the while. The small aging woman always worries about us not getting enough to eat at home because our family has to rely almost entirely on ration coupons. She knows that each child receives each week a portion of bread, butter, jam, and a few slices of sausage, amounts often small enough to be eaten in less than half that time. Each has a separate compartment in the pantry and, on our honor, we stay away from each other's rations. We have never gone hungry but often do not feel thoroughly satisfied; indulging ourselves to the point of complete satiation at one time would mean having to fast at another time.

The businessman's household knows fewer shortages because his customers from the country are often willing to add a little goodwill gift of food to the money and required purchase certificates for hard-to-get merchandise. From her own share at her employer's table, Heia reserves for our visits any good morsels that will not spoil.

I savor the cake and hot coffee and bask in the love of the old woman who wants to know every trivial detail of family news since my last visit. Heia always seems overly concerned, and by assuring her that all is well I sometimes make myself believe that it is. Occasionally I chafe under the excessive admonitions of Heia to whom I am still a little child to be guided and guarded; but at the same time I love the feeling of being pampered and cared for as by nobody else.

Since both of our boys have been drafted, her most anxious questions are always for news from them. Franz is still safely attached to a bicyclists' infantry unit in France and enjoying his often sought role as interpreter, which makes being a soldier more bearable to him. But Gerhard, after brief training at the Dutch border, is somewhere in Russia between Dnjepr and Donez heading into a troubled area. His last letter was a hastily penciled note with a special plea to Father:

"Vatel, I have a request you cannot deny me. Whenever you get mail from me, send word to Heidel so that she will not worry unduly."

Father made no comment, which to me implied his tacit approval that I could share all news from Gerhard with her. And in every letter since leaving home, Gerhard has told me to enjoy to the fullest what little fun comes my way, wishing he had made the most of his chances when he was still at home. As usual before I leave Heia, I promise to let her know immediately when we hear from one of the boys.

It is an unusual afternoon hour for Father to have returned from the office. When he fails to reply to my greeting, I walk up close to him just as he turns to face me. His stricken eyes cry out to me, and without a word he reaches for the open letter on the table, a letter like those so many others have received, the most dreaded letter the mailman has to deliver to any family. Gerhard is dead, eighteen-and-a-half and dead, the boy with adventure in his soul and enough ambition to reach for the stars—he is dead near Kharkov deep in Russia.

I cannot endure Father's look of utter desolation and flee to my room that was once Gerhard's. Too stunned to cry, I refuse to believe that he is dead. There is so much that I always wanted to tell him and never did, how much I admired him—his spunk, his determined response to any challenge— how flattered I was when he sincerely approved of Heiner, who asked me to the first ball, or when he would greet me with an almost courtly, old-fashioned bow and certain wave of his hand if we happened to pass on opposite sides of the street.

Here in this room, on the bed on which I now sit, I saw him on his last morning at home when I had to leave for school and he was relishing the remaining moments before departure. I did not ask him then what was on his mind, how he felt about leaving. And I did not give him the emotional good-bye hug that I felt tugging at my arms, for fear of offending his masculinity. How lonely and vulnerable he looked, devoid of the armor of bravado and levity and easy camaraderie that was his normal manner. Why had I failed him at this moment when I felt so close to him?

I recall one especially memorable time when I had also been quite alone with him, and he had not failed me. Tragedy had threatened the two of us together one summer at the Baltic Sea. He had learned to swim shortly before and was still far from equal to the risks of the unknown shore. We had discovered a wide sandbar, separated from the beach by a deep but narrow channel, no more than a dozen strokes to cross. We liked to play on the sandbar, and Father would carry me across the channel. Even then he insisted that I wear inflatable swim cushions, which protruded like wings from my back, because I had not learned to swim.

That day the sea was unusually restless and tossed us about, the roar of the waves swallowing our shrieks of delight and alarm. Suddenly the sandbar was gone from beneath my feet, leaving nothing but heaving water in all directions. Gerhard's head emerged close to mine, and he screamed to hang onto him and kick and yell. The waves had battered the air out of my swim cushions. I clung to him who was now struggling for both of us. Then Father's arms cut through a wave and, with a desperate push, propelled us toward the edge of a pier where alert observers of the near-tragedy pulled us up on the planks. That night in the dining room of our pension Gerhard basked in the accolades of our fellow guests, feeling quite the hero, and next morning he was back in the now becalmed vastness of water and sky, while I tripped cautiously at water's edge, running from every harmless ripple that threatened to wash against my legs.

If he had to die so young, we might as well have died together then. In this cruel hour, I wish we had.

Gerhard's daredevil spirit always kept him a jump ahead and a rock above the rest of us when Father took us mountain climbing. No wonder, then, that the wiry, lively boy was the only one in the family who ever suffered a broken bone! Was it his nature to test the limits in everything he undertook, or did he feel compelled by Father's expectations of what a boy should be? Was he trying to compensate, perhaps, for the intellectual, less exuberant older brother who had little affinity for Father's more extroverted interests? Father and Gerhard shared a love of soccer and shooting matches, and when not actively participating in sports, huddled by the radio to experience vicariously various championship events.

The two of them shared other bonds as well. Gerhard was the most appreciative listener when Father reminisced about his military career in the African colonies, and he knew the strange names of Herero chieftains and settlements better than any of us children. He enjoyed reenacting Father's tales with friends. When the African scene failed to entice them, he persuaded them to emulate heroes of Nordic sagas or characters, like Winnetou and Old Shatterhand, from the wild west yarns of Karl May.

Sometimes Gerhard's idea of fun got the best even of Father. Who but this mischievous boy would have dared sprinkle sneezing powder on Father's napkin and who could still grin while being chased around the dinner table by an irate, fitfully sneezing parent, certain to be dealt a rare, but well-deserved thrashing?

Father's determination to raise culturally well-rounded offspring foundered in one instance. To Gerhard fell the lot of taking violin lessons. For how long—a year or two—did the music teacher come to our house for this thankless task? At last the whole family rebelled against the screeching agony of these sessions and the daily practice until Father resigned himself to the fact that his second son had not been kissed by the muses.

Patience and discipline found other outlets for the boy who thrived on adventure. As a little general, he dispatched armies of tin soldiers to fight ancient wars over and over again, painstakingly moving formations of infantry and cavalry according to textbook diagrams and imitating the sound of bugles and the noise of battle. He had won so many wars then, but now lost the only battle that mattered, a brave, little, anonymous tin soldier at another general's mercy.

The thoughts and images flash relentlessly through my mind as I try to grasp the finality of the terse official communication.

Father walks quietly into the room, reaching for me and drawing me close. Then he looks at me and says slowly:

"I think you should go and tell Fräulein Heidel." It is the only time since Heia left us that he admits knowing that his children, defying him, had remained close to her and always would.

Without giving a thought to what I will say to her and

unaware of how I got to her door, I ring the bell above the hardware store. No words are needed when Heia opens the door and sees me standing there. She whispers:

"Gerhard?"

In each other's arms we cry together and cling to each other against the terrible blow that each has secretly feared and now has to suffer.

"Today is your Mama's birthday," she sobs. "God was merciful to spare her this day."

The family, Heia, and a few close friends attend a requiem for our first dead of the war. In the aisle before the altar stands an empty sarcophagus draped in black. On top of it lie a pair of crossed sabers and a soldier's helmet. The body of the brother I learned to love too late lies dead in a foreign grave on the Russian plain.

Weeks later Father receives a small package with Gerhard's personal possessions. In it are diary notes he had intended to send and had asked to have safely stored until he came home, or destroyed unread if he did not, a few letters and items without value.

"That's all that is left of him," says Father, breaking down at last. To me he gives a letter from a girl whom Gerhard had met away from home, and the task to write her of his death. Reluctantly, but honor-bound by Gerhard's request, we burn the diaries which could have preserved for us a glimmer of his soul.

In town I can't avoid meeting one or another of Gerhard's friends home on leave. I can hardly restrain myself from shouting: "How can you be well and safe when he is dead?" But aren't they, too, already marked for death? Isn't that what a soldier's uniform means?

One by one, we receive back the letters we had sent to Gerhard that never reached him, each of them a confirmation that he is no more.

The routine of our days continues outwardly uninterrupted. Father even encourages me to resume dancing lessons:

"Go ahead with it, my girl, we can't be sad forever.

Nothing can bring him back," he says. "And hasn't he told you often enough to have a good time while you can?"

Sometimes I don't feel like dancing, but sometimes in the depth of grief I am overcome by a sudden surge of hunger for lights and laughter and music that I want to dance until I am unconscious, to snatch at happiness, and to forget what has happened and what may still be ahead.

Civilian War Service

The shrill signal of the alarm clock tears through the silence. Hard it is, indeed, to get up when no one else is moving about in the apartment and the indistinct shadows of dawn still shroud my room. But I must not be late for the train.

Moving quietly through the hall, I feel the chill of the August morning through my thin gown and hurry to close the bathroom window. The cold shower is a small victory and an affirmation that I am my Father's daughter; he braves this chilly onslaught with shouts of aversion and defiance every day of the year. Toweling my tingling body dry, I shed the remnants of sleep and reluctance from body and mind. While having a cup of "coffee" made from flavored roasted grain and a slice of bread for breakfast on the run, I slip into my *BDM* uniform, ready to face the new day.

The hesitant light of day grows stronger as I walk to the passenger station near the center of town. Even at this hour the station is not deserted. It never is, since every train day or night brings soldiers home on leave or takes them away, or spills refugees loaded with bundles on the platform on their way to uncertain safety.

I am the first to arrive and anxiously scan the square outside the building for a sign of the girls I am to supervise in our first assignment in the armament industry. Within minutes about thirty of them report to receive their train passes.

"What do you think we will be doing?"

"Do you know where the plant is located?"

All are full of questions about the day ahead of us, but I know little more than anyone else.

"We will get off the train in Mittelsteine. Let's hope someone from Patin will meet us."

When we arrive, a representative from the airplane parts plant, which has been relocated from the endangered city of Berlin to our relatively safe mountain country, is expecting us on this first morning. During the fifteen-minute walk from the station we get an inkling of what our responsibilities will be as checkers in the plant. When the guarded gate closes behind us, we are issued identification passes and time cards.

A section head in a white laboratory coat addresses us in a brief welcoming speech, which is prefaced and studded throughout and summed up with stern reminders that we are now a part of the Greater German war effort, that the fatherland depends on us, and that our obligation is as binding as the loyalty oath of a soldier. Intimidated and feeling trapped more than inspired, we follow him into a low-ceilinged, brightly-lit room in which women are already at work, lined up on both sides along rows of long, narrow tables. Each of us is assigned a chair at one of the tables on which boxes with small metal parts are set out. With each different type of metal part goes a testing tool. The section head shows us how to slip this tool into or over the part to be checked and how to determine whether a part is to be accepted or rejected.

Work begins. The room is quiet except for the tiny clink of metal upon metal. When one box is completely tested and sorted into passing and defective parts, another is brought immediately, and so on in never-ending flow. The only distraction is the occasional change in the shape of parts and the design of the testing tool for that particular shape. All we know is that the screw which passes our inspection will some day be buried in some mechanism of an airplane body which a German pilot will fly somewhere against the enemy.

Even the most highly motivated have to fight against the tedium induced by the sameness of the motion of our hands. The work is easier than we had imagined, and much duller.

The hours pass slowly, and every day thereafter is much like the first.

The work day is strictly scheduled. The same group of workers takes a break in the morning and in the afternoon at exactly the same time every day. At lunchtime we file into a cheerless hall, which serves as cafeteria, to receive in stacked mess kits ladles full of meager wartime stew or soup, perhaps a salad, and a slice of bread. For this we surrender precious ration coupons by the week.

Although the plant consists of several buildings, we have access only to our workroom, the cafeteria, and a small courtyard in which we can walk during breaks. Once on an errand for the section head, I blunder into a machine room where men in greasy overalls are working. When I ask one of them for directions, he answers in a language reminiscent of and yet different from my school French. The plant, it turns out, employs male foreign labor and German women, with only a few German men in supervisory positions.

Breaks and mealtimes are arranged so that workers from different areas of the operation should not meet. Yet occasionally in the courtyard, a few moments variation in the schedule of a group can be a revelation. Primitive toilet shacks have been constructed on several sides. Opposite from where we usually stand and walk, a dismal lot of people in loose-fitting drab garments are lined up outside one of the latrines. Their heads are shaved and their faces haggard. A stout woman in *SS* uniform shouts to them to get moving, while another pushes some shrieking people from the shack. Attracted by the commotion, we watch and listen. The exchange between the pitiful creatures and the uniformed women is all in German. In a flash of recognition, the situation becomes clear: A group of Jewish women, some of them no older than we, is denied the time to relieve themselves. They are herded back to work without mercy or dignity. The scene, which we were not meant to see, remains etched in our minds, raising terrifying questions about rumored inhumanities, about frightening stories that from time to time one hears whispered.

Only a few years ago I sat side by side in school with the daughters of Jewish merchants and doctors. They left school for no apparent reason, all at about the same time. Is this, or worse perhaps, what has happened to them?

One monotonous day follows another, beginning with the train ride on ever-darker mornings and ending with the train ride home after an exhausting, boring day at the inspection tables. The idea of total war and service to the fatherland is stripped of all glamor, and unfathomable thoughts of right and wrong are troubling us. But *discipline* and *sacrifice* are the key words for everyone in those days, and they triumph over a nagging sense of inescapable involvement and unease.

I still take roll call at the station every morning and count all present without fail. When I come home in the evening, I am tired and often depressed because there is nothing to look forward to. Rarely do I see one of my friends; they are just as busy and tired from their assignments as I am. Our boy friends, as a school class with their teachers, are stationed as *Luftwaffenhelfer* ("Air Force Auxiliary") somewhere in the east until they are old enough for the draft. Rudi, who emerged as my favorite dancing partner and steady of sorts and who tormented me no end with other flirtations, exists only in long letters, such good, serious letters that bring him closer to me than he has ever been. One more to write to—so many pen pals and no one to talk and laugh with.

My first walk when I come home is always to check for mail under my pillow. Regardless of who has written or what, then I can feel sure that one of my soldiers is still alive, or was at the time of writing. Some letters are mere scraps of paper, scribbled on by insufficient light in cramped quarters, but they are for me truly a sign of life. Alfons's, my sailor's, last letter gave me a shock at first because it came from a field hospital, but then I was almost happy because his wound will keep him safe for weeks to come.

Home has become a subdued place, except for the presence of my little sister, whose school life continues unchanged and who is full of excitement over her budding interest in boys. She can almost do as she pleases—Father was much

48

stricter with me at her age. I still can't look at him without a stab of pain, at how much he has aged since Gerhard's death. His black hair is graying rapidly, and his cheekbones stand out prominently in his haggard and lackluster face. He is seldom at home because his office demands ever-longer hours to compensate for the absence of younger colleagues in the military service. Mother, too, looks weary after a day at the troop trains and seems shrunken and more quiet than ever. Sometimes she brings a stranger home who has been stranded in transit without quarters for the night. Not even counting soldiers, so many people are traveling, but there are no accommodations left in town. The military takes priority in everything, and lately an influx of refugees has swamped our safe haven where no bomb has yet fallen.

Our maid won't be with us much longer because for our family without small children she is considered dispensable, and she has orders to report to the army hospital auxiliary. Being among all those soldiers will be her cup of tea, I thought at first; but she doesn't like the idea of having to go, and we don't like to have her leave us.

For a few weeks I had to surrender my room to Hans-Georg, a twelve-year-old, whose school was evacuated from Breslau. Frequent air raids there disrupted classes too often and at night cheated the children of their sleep, making effective teaching impossible. He was such a quiet boy that we hardly knew he was here, but he got homesick and returned to his parents, school or no school.

Sometimes the way we now live seems unreal, as if we were marionettes, with orders and permits and schedules attached to us instead of strings. From the time we are old enough to be of any use, we are hooked to a machine called "total war," and even those too young can't escape its effect.

Reprieve

Another industrial operation has been moved into our old town in the mountains. German army prisoners previously quartered in the grim buildings of the fortress have been shipped to the Eastern Front to serve, what time is granted to them, in clearing mine fields and ridding the area of partisans before the retreating troops. Now scientific personnel of one of the largest national electronics firms supervise the conversion of the camouflaged fortress and its subterranean spaces into the new home for laboratories and manufacturing operations. While people in supervising and managing positions are imported with the plant, local manpower must provide the workers.

A mathematics teacher from our school recruits students with a good record in mathematics and physics to be trained for laboratory work, I among them. What a relief to be called away from the airplane parts plant with its troubling visions of the Jewish women and foreign laborers! Besides, I can sleep till a decent hour every morning and wear civilian clothes.

The next few weeks seem like a return to the classroom. Every morning we climb the hill to the Army Communications Center, where an electronics engineer lectures on the laws of electricity and teaches us the intricacies of electrical instrumentation. Physics is no longer mere observation of interesting experiments but a real-life challenge. But for some of us the intellectual stimulation is temporary, and the newly gained knowledge serves no useful purpose. Induction orders from the *Reichsarbeitsdienst* ("National Labor Service") are due to call the seventeen-year-olds to camps away from home.

This organization was established as a compulsory service for all seventeen- and eighteen-year-old men and women and designed to swell the work force with young people, assigning city youths to farms and public-labor projects and bringing country youths into urban environments. One year was required of all physically fit. The manpower needs of the war reduced the traditional camp life to half a year, after which the young women were assigned to armament industry and hospital work, and the young men exchanged the olive drab of the *RAD* for the uniforms of the armed services. In the latter part of the war, the half-year was further reduced for the women and frequently omitted for the men, many of whom—like the boys from Glatz— were ordered at an even earlier age as students to quasi-military service while being taught by accompanying teachers between their supportive military duties.

The graduating class of my school gathers for a farewell party in a local restaurant. It is the last time we meet as a group before being caught up in the machinery of a highly organized state and for many the last time ever. The few whom physical disability defers or excuses from induction are the only ones who will remain with their families and work in local war projects. The fate of the others rides on the whims of orders beyond our own or our parents' control.

Since I had to report for the preinduction physical examination, the days are reduced to waiting. A feeling of suspension makes every activity unreal and meaningless. I still attend the electronics training classes, without caring whether the firm's application for deferment will be granted or not. Although I want the medical reports to declare me perfectly fit and would feel inferior if they did not, I am not looking forward to camp life and what else may be in store. Without having any say in the matter of my future, all I want to know is where and when.

Then the paralyzing uncertainty is over. My orders to report to a never-heard-of location in Czechoslovakia even kindle a spark of anticipation for traveling to a foreign country, being among new people, moving toward new experiences whatever they might be. I begin to sort through my clothes, books, and personal treasures, realizing how little I will be able to take along, and yet I am reluctant to pack them away: I don't want to give up my place in house and family sooner than necessary. Every activity and every meeting is a small farewell. Old family friends to whom I say good-bye regard me with open concern because my destination is rumored to be infested with partisans. They say that Germans are considered enemies in annexed territories, except among the native German contingent in the borderland

and isolated ethnic islands. Surely they worry needlessly, but I am touched by their concern.

Family tradition calls for attending mass before setting out on any journey or other serious undertaking. Afterwards, the farewell at home is brief and unemotional. Father is off on a military training course for older men, and Annemie is at school. No one else matters.

Two other girls from my school are bound for camps in the same general direction but each to a different location. No old ties are allowed to interfere in the planned mingling of young people from different backgrounds and hometowns, so to be molded into cohesive units. While the train carries us for hours in a southeasterly direction, we chat as if bound for a vacation until first one, then the other must go her separate way.

Reichsarbeitsdienst (RAD)

Girls from all over eastern Germany have arrived and now trudge over slushy country roads, feeling the surrounding isolation grow heavier with every kilometer. My apprehensions of what the camp would look like are eased when we spot the flag that identifies a large stone building as our destination. From a gentle rise, the former Czech school looks down on distant small villages and fields covered with the first snow of winter. The violence and noise of the times belong to another world, not even the roar of trains reaches into the sleepy silence because the closest railroad lies kilometers behind us.

Within hours we are issued uniforms and linens and assigned to bunks, about twelve to a room. The whiteness outside brightens the high-ceilinged sleeping rooms, the tall windows having no drapes covering them. In separate rooms, the few remnants of our former lives are confined to lockers, along with a complete outfit of dress and work clothes, from boots to woolen caps, shoulder bags to underwear. But even the lockers will not remain entirely private territory because they are subject to inspection. Dressed in olive-drab suits with earth-brown collars cloaking our various origins with anonymity, we have been transformed into *RAD-Maiden*, ready to become acquainted with our leaders and the layout of the camp.

At the head of the hierarchy of leaders stands a tall woman who is the daughter of a German professor at Prague university, married to an *SS* officer and expecting his child. She holds a position of authority and maintains a formal distance. She and her assistants occupy comfortable private rooms. The leaders on the lowest level are assigned one to each sleeping room, in constant direct contact with us girls and in charge of the so-called *Kameradschaften*. Kitchen, laundry, and showers are located in the basement. In the quiet wing where the leaders live there is also a medical dispensary and small infirmary.

Meals are served in a large common room which doubles as classroom, music room, sports and assembly hall, and sewing room; in short, it is the scene of all communal activity, and there is rarely any but communal activity. Within days—during meals, in brief exchanges in locker rooms, during house and kitchen duties—girls of similar mind and like background find each other. The artificial depersonalization lasts only as long as everyone is a stranger among strangers; it is quickly overcome by budding personal alliances.

After a week's confinement in camp, having been drilled, lectured, and taught the rudimentary skills and rules of conduct, we are ready for the rural labor program. Early as on every morning, the flag-raising ceremony finds the whole camp assembled outdoors. Then small groups move off in all directions to the German farms, while other groups, alternating by the week, stay in camp for kitchen, laundry, and other housekeeping duties. There is no shirking work in or out of camp, but most girls prefer contact with the farm families and unfamiliar winter chores to the sterile atmosphere and the closely supervised work at camp.

I am fortunate in my first assignment. It lands me in the lap of abundance on a large, wealthy, modern farm in the area, belonging to a party dignitary. As an agricultural teaching facility, this farm is populated by a few *Landwirtschafts-lehrlingen* ("agricultural trainees") in addition to field hands and other workers. Two girls who are in a phase of training in which they learn to run a large rural household become my companions and mentors. Friendly and boisterous, they tease me about my ignorance of the chores they do with ease, performing what appear to me culinary feats while I observe in admiration.

"Before you leave here, you will know how to turn out a proper apple strudel," they promise. "Just remember to fold and roll the dough until it is thin enough to read the newspaper through it."

Time after time I fail miserably. Since I can neither match their facility with brooms and pressing irons, they leave me the simplest tasks, such as setting the table and washing dishes and the like. Several days I spend in the fruit cellar examining the apple crop which is spread out on neatly stacked wooden slats in single layers. Any fruit that is less than perfect is sorted out for immediate use. My conscience remains undisturbed when some luscious rejects are consumed on the spot.

Like me, almost all the girls from camp enjoy the hearty meals served on the farms and learn to ignore what amounts to our servant status. After years of subsisting on ration diets in the cities, we blossom into robust young women whose physical well-being counters surges of hurt pride and resentment and periods of homesickness.

Work in camp is a greater challenge to me because no one is allowed to fail there. After I have scrubbed one of the unpolished floors without, to me, satisfactory results, a more savvy comrade points out that the first principle of cleaning is *Staubverteilung*, and I embrace with relief the idea that dirt and dust distributed evenly looks clean enough. With trepidation I tackle the job of building fires in the tile stoves with a minimum of waste paper and kindling. When the coals finally begin to glow, I feel like a minor Prometheus.

Sometimes when we gather in the evenings at camp for

singing and folk dancing, we forget our involuntary service and let high spirits reign; we learn to live for the present, for one day at a time. Once the camp commander's sister, who has fled from a bombarded city and lives quietly and privately at camp, treats a few of us who are interested to a reading of Rilke's *Cornet*. I am so captivated by its romance and sadness that I learn it by heart. From the time of the recitation on, I search my memory for every verse ever learned and fill the dullness of solitary chores with silently recited words of lasting beauty. The gamut of emotions they express transcends the present, letting my mind and body lead a secret double life. No one can invade the private territory I have discovered in myself.

Three-Day Pass

Mail call is the high point of each day. For a fleeting interlude, each girl becomes once again an individual immersed in private thoughts and concerns, secret smiles and sorrows. The last letter from home has turned for me the daily humdrum into anguish and hope.

Dear little Gina,
How very painful it was for me to find you no longer at home when I arrived yesterday slightly wounded. . . .

Wounded at the western front, Franz has contrived to be transferred to a hometown hospital and to live at home while receiving out-patient treatment.

. . . Hoping that you will be able to escape for a few days and that I will still be here waiting for you, I greet a thousand times my poor sister in exile,

Franz.

Franz at home—I must see him! And no power on earth will keep me away!

The oldest of the children, five years older than I, Franz

has been my favorite playmate, protector, soul mate for as far back as I can remember. When we were very young, we planned our lives together: He would become a priest or professor in keeping with his early obvious inclination to solitude and scholarship, and I would be his companion and housekeeper. We invented a language for our infantile games with cuddly teddy bears, and remnants from it carried over into private endearments long after the toys had gone limp with age and become mere keepsakes. In a family not given to shows of emotion and affection, Franz was the gentle exception, and he poured his tenderness on me, his favorite little sister. Later we shared an interest in music and in foreign languages and literature, and had dreams of traveling all over the world together. Ironically, his first trip to a foreign country was in a soldier's uniform in an enterprise diametrically opposed to his nature, and now I, in another uniform, am stationed in the Protectorate of Bohemia and Moravia, also a foreign country until in the Greater German expansion in 1938 it ceased to be Czechoslovakia.

From France, where Franz was assigned, he sent to me the flowered silk and the filmy georgette for dancing dresses when the fabric shops in Germany had depleted their prewar stock, and the silk stockings and perfume that made me feel so grown up and pretty when our class from the girls' school attended dancing lessons with the next higher class from the boys' school.

I was always waiting for Franz to come home and if he merely mentioned the prospect of a leave, would wish for it with desperate determination, believing that I could make it happen. Sometimes for days at a time I would invent errands to coincide with train schedules and day after day would meet trains from the west, expecting each to bring him at last, and would picture his surprise and delight to find me waiting. Of course, it never happened this way. Meanwhile we bridged the separation with a multilingual correspondence. Abiding by his rules, I faithfully responded in the same language— French, English, or German respectively—in which his letters were written.

The door bell rang one afternoon when I was idly entertaining myself on the piano with Strauss tunes, and no one else was at home. The "caller" was my weary and heavily laden brother. Within moments he shed bags and uniform and in my place finished the interrupted waltz we both loved, celebrating his homecoming.

He detested the uniform he had to wear and any other uniform, but to flatter my teenage vanity, the handsome young officer would don his field-gray for a stroll through town together. Best of all were the trips to the theater and opera just for the two of us. On evenings at home he could spark conversations with his wit and inject my dull homework with little-known anecdotes about people and places gleaned from his extensive reading. But the times when the whole family could idle away long evenings have become increasingly rare. What a delight long ago Franz's recitations of Wilhelm Busch's rhymes had been or his reading of Thoma's *Lausbubengeschichten*, which we came to know almost by heart and still asked for over and over again!

Words, whether in literature or in conversation, were his delight as well as his weapon. Impeccable in his personal habits, he abhorred disorder and sloppiness. Our charming but flighty sister Annemie was often the target of his mock-harangues. With a slight shift of the accent to the last syllable, *Annemie* became *Anaemie* or *perniziöse Anaemie* whenever she kindled his wrath, and his mere mouthing of the uncomplimentary epithet, although beyond her comprehension, would send her shrieking to Father for aid against the disapproving brother.

Franz's imagination was always at work, whether in childish drawings or in the pursuit of other people's flights of fancy in the books he devoured, whether in solitude or in play with companions. When the games of cards or "school," in which he challenged our knowledge, began to pall, he invented new ones and then created the boards and simple utensils to make them work. His games of chance for nuts and candy entertained the family through many a long winter evening.

But no toy or hobby could ever compete with his electric train. On it his imagination traversed the continents and grew ever more eager for learning about strange places which he meant to explore some day. His excitement and enthusiasm swept me along on trips into fantasy land which, as I grew older, emerged as the existing world, and no longer unattainable but for the turn of political events.

And now Franz is at home, and I am condemned to being a drudge and to being regimented by camp rules far from home! Since my first request for leave was not rejected with an unqualified no, I hope wildly from day to day for a decision in my favor. Visiting a wounded soldier, my only remaining brother, is deemed a war-related family matter, deserving of a three-day pass. By the time this word reaches me, Christmas is only two weeks away—would it be worth waiting a little longer to spend the holidays with Franz and the family? I leave the decision to Franz. It comes by return mail, briefer than any letter he has ever written to me:

> Sweet little idiot,
> Never postpone a leave. Who knows where we will be by Christmas! Come immediately! Wolfgang happens to be on leave and wants to see you, too.
>
> > Impatiently,
> > your brother Franz.

Come immediately—if only I could, I would start out this instant! But the bureaucratic process which has already been set in motion, now backed by proper documentation from home, takes time to complete, and only the final signature can set me free.

When I board the train two days later, I still have not resolved the problem of Mozart, which has been Wolfgang's nickname since we were childhood playmates, a tribute to his musical talent. I am determined not to spare him or anyone else a moment of my precious three days at home with Franz. And yet, how can I refuse to see Mozart without feeling guilty? His last letter months ago was all but illegible, scribbled in pencil in a frontline trench, amid crouching men, weapons, and excrement—how I had recoiled at his explicit reference to these conditions, not wishing to acknowledge them as they really were. How disgusting they must have been for him to mention them at all! Being wounded and away from there must have come as a relief.

Hardly has the glow of reunion subsided at home, when all of them, and Franz most emphatically, insist that we invite Mozart, even if only for a few hours between trains from and to Waldenburg near where he lives. Squirm and resist as I might, I at last agree to call him. His leave has been canceled abruptly, tells his mother tearfully, and he is on his way back to the front. I have my way and my deserved portion of shame, as though I had caused his recall.

Three days pass in a blur of the pleasant feel of clothes that are not government owned, of too few long evenings of Father's hospitality that does not stop with one glass of wine and one cigarette this time, and every daytime hour together with Franz. He applies for a travel permit to take me all the way back to camp but is turned down. Early on the third morning, I once again in my olive drab and Franz in his field gray, we walk to the train station. For a parting gift he hands me a pack of cigarettes "to celebrate the holidays in captivity," and we cling together till the conductor's whistle.

3

Sic Transit Gloria Mundi

Retreat

The unthinkable has become commonplace. Almost daily enemy planes fly over the wintry countryside, but the sirens remain silent or too distant to hear; no matter, there is nowhere to go for safety. Once a damaged plane totters dangerously low over the camp, releasing a few bundles that billow into parachutes with men dangling from them before it goes down, down, out of sight. No bombs fall from the sky because there are no worthwhile targets in this remote land. Now and then detonations on the ground signal the increasing activity of saboteurs.

The camp staff has contrived to make the Christmas season truly festive and harmonious. On the long winter evenings we handcraft table and tree decorations out of wood and paper, make needlework gifts for each other, while listening to stories of Christmases past and singing carols. The smell of baking wafts from the kitchen, mingling with the fumes of coal fires and wax candles. On Christmas Eve, lights-out is scheduled early for a nap before the festivities begin. Shortly before midnight, excited like children, we assemble in dress uniforms in the hall outside the common room. While we slept, the leaders have trimmed a floor-to-ceiling spruce, set the tables for a festive meal, and arranged presents on the wall around the room. The magic of Christmas has invaded the camp and now invades our hearts.

Packages and letters have been saved for days to climax our joy this evening. Among my gifts are *Ein Weihnachtsmärchen* and a slim volume of poems by Walther Flex from Father, my share of the family's meager lot of Christmas sweets, and, best of all, a note from Franz that closes, "with my best and most deeply felt wishes for the New Year I embrace you and remain yours ever loving, Franz."

In spite of the temporary distraction of holiday activities, I ache with homesickness. Franz's cigarettes are the only tangible proof of my days with him. In unguarded moments in the evenings, I stand before the open fire door of the tile stove to disguise the smoke, inhaling each puff as though it were Franz's breath, and hide my lurking tears behind the bravado it takes to defy camp rules.

Since Christmas a mood of restless expectancy has spread like a contagion through the camp. Among the girls on assignment in one of the larger villages, I see the first troops since coming to camp, a long straggling line of infantry, moving, hardly marching, on the main road through the area. They are remnants of the Vlasov Army—anti-Stalinist Russian soldiers who fought for Germany under General Andreé A. Vlasov—and the sight of the weary armed men, who wear German uniforms but are not German soldiers, is vaguely disquieting, as if presaging the coming of other strange soldiers in enemy uniforms.

When mail call passes without a letter from home, worry becomes despair. Each of us lives in a private hell in which fear for our own safety is the least hard to bear. Franz's convalescent leave has been cut short, and given the choice between rejoining his unit in the west or assignment to another close to home, he has opted for transfer to the Eastern Front, which is moving ever closer to home.

The Eastern Front has become a jagged line from the Baltic Sea to the Balkan countries, with a number of wedges driven across the German border, and one of these is reported to aim in the direction of Slovakia, toward us. Now it has come to pass that our lives are in serious danger. Mines have exploded in neighboring villages, and still we wait, wait. A storm of fire and destruction is sweeping toward us, toward home. My eyes after sleepless nights smart as if from the smoke of burning towns. If I should lose everything I hold dear, I would not want to live.

The evenings at camp are filled with preparations for sudden departure. We pack our personal belongings in the suitcases brought from home, keeping only uniforms and needed toiletries in our lockers. From heavy blankets we are instructed to fashion huge backpacks in which each can carry the issued outfits and a share of the camp supplies. The act of packing is therapeutic because always before it has been in preparation of some adventure or fun-filled vacation or at the end of one before returning to a secure and familiar routine. Even now it gives me relief. Being in danger like those at home, like Franz and Father, makes me one of them.

Each meal is a feast because it might be the last one, and the need to economize has ceased. With luxurious abandon, we enjoy daily hot showers, the hot water never running out as there is coal to waste in a short time that was meant to last all winter. The work routine of the day continues. The camp must maintain a semblance of normality to quiet the growing panic among the German civilian population.

Nearly a week passes without incident or marching orders, while news gets worse by the day. Battles are in progress between Namslau and Oels, in the very area where Father had to report for a "training exercise," and the Silesian capital of Breslau is within shelling distance of Russian artillery. What is happening to Father, and what to Marianne and her family on the outskirts of Breslau?

I leave camp on skis on a crisp, snowy morning, momentarily letting my spirit soar in the exhilarating downhill run to the farm where I am on duty. A picture-postcard day outdoors, it turns into a storybook day in the cozy farm kitchen. The womenfolk of the neighborhood have gathered to pluck down for stuffing pillows and huge featherbeds for some bride's trousseau. While the pots on the coal stove are humming and bubbling, we chatter comfortably and giggle under our breath when the fine feathers tickle someone into a hearty sneeze. Our head scarves are as white as if the snow from outside had drifted over them, lending the robust faces of the young and the wrinkled ones of the old women a common look of age. I feel in the middle of one of Mama's tales from her childhood come alive.

Into this fairytale scene, a messenger from camp throws reality like a bomb:

"We have been ordered to evacuate. Report immediately."

She rushes on to alert others. Now that the camp is moving, the farm women know that they, too, are in danger. A few start crying because the farewell from me whom they have just begun to know may be the first of many farewells and worse to come. Once more a cross-country run on skis back to camp. In my desperate haste, my sense of time has gone awry and is playing tricks on me. What if I were to lose my way in the glaring whiteness and were left behind?

Hurried last-minute packing, then the long march through the snow to the train station. Our destination is another camp deep in central Czechoslovakia; there is nowhere left to run but southwest. The layovers at the larger stations vividly illustrate what has happened to others and what may lie ahead for us. Soldiers are everywhere, some coming straight from the front in Upper Silesia with tales more desolate than any news we have yet heard, others heading toward the front, grim and resigned. Wounded in ragged uniforms, one supporting another, drag through the halls in search of the Red Cross sign. The waiting rooms overflow onto drafty platforms with women surrounded by awkward bundles, old men trying to calm crying little children and shield them in their arms from the bitter wind. Among the homeless, the hopeless, the fatalistic, a few stroll whose features and language betray their belief that judgment is at hand at last, and deservedly, and that they are immune and will triumph in the end—as if anyone could escape unscathed in the impending chaos.

Exhausted sleep on the night train to Brünn and the luxury of a well-tended waiting room there make the earlier phase of the trip seem like a nightmare. At last we unload in a small station near Iglau.

The first sight of the new camp makes us long for the one we had to leave. Primitive wooden barracks, crowded to overflowing, and an overtaxed staff that shows signs of frustration at the influx of refugees awaits us. Instead of having the convenience of a whole community under one roof, we now wade through slush and mud from our quarters to the common rooms. Tired and disheartened, we welcome the prospect of immediate assignment to farm work. The less time spent in this camp, the better we will like it.

Bohemian Idyll

Once again the visions of a world at war are blotted out. It is only February, but the air carries a hint of spring, and the long walk into the village is a blissful reminder of many jubilant early spring strolls at home. The farm to which I report is a sprawling group of whitewashed buildings above a stream. If the yard and the buildings look well-kept and spotless, the large kitchen as well is a model of cleanliness in an old-fashioned, rough-hewn way. An enormous stove dominates it, without a speck of coal dust soiling the white-scrubbed, unpolished wood floor beyond the metal apron by the fire door. Pots hanging on the wall and dishes in the carved cupboards sparkle. An impeccable starched cloth covers the smaller of two tables; the other, larger, one is bare wood and flanked by benches.

For once I am glad of my work uniform—a bright blue linen dress, red head scarf, and coarsely woven dark green apron—because it seems to blend in with the costume the women wear. The matriarch, who is the obvious head of the household in the absence of her son in military service, is a stout old woman. Over a white blouse she wears a tight-fitting black bodice and gathered skirt; when she bends down or walks in an agile, resolute, hip-swinging way, the skirt whips around her sturdy legs in white stockings, revealing the bright red skirt lining and the embroidered frills of white bloomers. Her daughter-in-law, a child-woman, is dressed in a similar costume in less severe colors; stiff braids are pulled tightly back beneath the edge of a head scarf and held together with a tiny bow in her nape.

How stiff my literary German sounds against the lilting dialect these people speak! I feel out of place and would like to look and listen rather than participate and talk. But the matriarch is curious about this new member of her household and asks direct questions. She labels me a "studied" person. This pronouncement is so inscrutable that I cannot tell whether the old woman is impressed or being deprecative.

Whatever her secret thoughts, she expects work well done. I scrub the already clean floors until my arms ache and my knees feel calloused. I rinse the wash in the icy water of the stream. In the root cellar I scrape caked soil from turnips and potatoes, cheering myself up by thinking of my discovery on the cellar steps. A big crockery jar stands there full of milk on which the cream has risen to a thick layer. On the way down, when my hands are still clean, I can trail a finger over the top and lick the richest delicacy I have tasted in years. My aversion to the root cellar melts away in visions of long-ago strawberry tarts heaped with whipped cream.

Crisis comes at dinner time. The small table is set for two. Along with a bread knife and several spoons, a large bowl of goulash in cream sauce and a hunk of bread are placed on the large table. As the servants are coming in, the matriarch and the young woman sit down at the small table. I remain undecided until urged to sit on one of the benches at the large table. Each of the servants takes a spoon and goes to work on the goulash, alternately dipping slices of bread into the rich gravy. I cannot bring myself to do the same. With a chuckle, the matriarch leaves her chair, ladles an ample plateful from the pot on the stove, and sets it in front of me. Then I can enjoy dinner as much as any of them.

In the short period on this farm, I come to look for

65

flashes of humor on the broad, kind face that reminds me of a favorite elderly relative, but I never feel quite at ease with the old woman and her distrust of city people or with the reticence of the young woman hardly older than I. Most agreeable is the work indoors and out in the company of a boisterous servant girl. Ours is an uncomplicated relationship, a simple sharing of the work at hand. Uncritical of my ineptness at some of the activities that seem to come naturally to her, she enjoys being my teacher and I pretend to be her understudy in an idyllic pastoral play.

Promotion

The days in camp are numbered. Only four months after induction into the regular *RAD*, we face the second phase of service which will tear us out of the now familiar community and scatter us singly or in small groups throughout the constantly shrinking confines of Greater Germany. All assignments will propel us directly into the monstrous machinery of the war which, already slowing down, grinds on desperately and inexorably.

Potential leaders have been singled out and, predictably, girls with advanced schooling make up the majority of the selected group. Weeks ago the leader of our first camp had approached a few of us to suggest leadership training. I had stalled her uncomfortably, saying that I would have to think about it, although I had no intention of tying my life to the *RAD* any longer than the minimal compulsory year. This time it is not a matter of choice but of orders, and it does not mean duty in a regular *RAD* camp but heading a *Kriegsdienst* ("war service") unit. For our specific assignments we are to report to the district headquarters in Brünn. We respond to the prospect of a day away from camp with the enthusiasm which we lack for the purpose of the trip. No matter what it might reveal, a firsthand look at the world outside is better than being cut off and imagining the worst. Here, deep in the heart of Czechoslovakia, nothing seems changed since the trip from our former camp; the occasional flashes in the night sky and the distant rumble of bombardments are still too far away to be threatening. The trains are not crowded, and the station in Brünn still has a look of normalcy about it.

Each of us has a secret wish for a particular assignment in the new leadership role but also the certain and frustrating knowledge that the impending orders are a matter of luck rather than personal preference. For me the most desirable possibility is service in an army hospital in Prague. The attraction is twofold: If I must be active in support of the war, I want to counteract the violence by caring for its most exposed victims, even if it means only to ease their dying. Destruction that tumbles cities and devastates countries, monstrous though it is, seems insignificant to me measured against the ruins of human lives. Material objects have no body to writhe in pain and no soul to recoil in horror. I never could bear the sight of suffering and illness, but now I long to be part of it all in order to try to alleviate it. And I will not turn away as I did from the quadruple amputee in my hometown hospital. The second of Prague's attractions seems so frivolous, I am almost ashamed to admit it to myself. It is the Golden City of my dreams, a center of beauty and culture, now the last one virtually untouched in central Europe: Here I might find satisfaction for my nostalgic hunger for the civilized life that the war is snatching from my grasp; just being there might give me a glance at a past which I can no longer believe will endure in the future.

From the group that left camp together, a few of us are called into a conference room at headquarters.

"Where are you from?" a leader asks each in turn. As if she had not known the answers beforehand, she states:

"Silesians all. Your homeland is in grave danger, and I think that I can speak for all of you that you would want to take part in its defense against the Russians. The success of our brave *Wehrmacht* depends for vital supplies on unafraid women like you. We must keep their guns blazing to halt the enemy."

They are throwing us to the wolves! We had been evacuated to be safe, and now we are being sent to an area much more endangered than the camp we left. This makes no sense!

As we "volunteers" stand in stunned silence, she passes out individual orders. These read: *Munitionsdepot* Landeshut, Schlesien.

Dismissed and out of earshot, we vent our suppressed reactions.

"They can't do that to us!"

"Unafraid women! Suddenly we are women!"

"Unafraid? I am scared, aren't you?"

"At least we will be closer to home."

"We will literally be sitting on a powder keg."

"I would rather have a gun and fight than be blown skyhigh."

"Where is the front anyway?"

"Calm down, everybody," chuckles someone. "A week from now when we have to report, the place will already be blown up and we can simply go home."

Nobody laughs. If we still have a home to go to—the frightening thought that I have tried to hold at bay for weeks is suddenly written on every face around me.

As I lie on my bunk that night, I am more disappointed than upset or afraid. Goodbye, Golden City, which I will never see! Goodbye, noble dreams of healing! I never wanted to hurt anyone. How do soldiers feel when they must kill? Does work in a munitions factory make a person a killer?

Night

March 16, 1945, the second anniversary of Gerhard's death in Russia. Few days have passed in the past two years in which thoughts of him have not surfaced, and the dull ache of irretrievable loss never quite leaves me. It is all one now with the gloom that even the most stouthearted can no longer resist nor conceal. More than usual, some undefined trouble makes me restless and ill at ease. I found a trace of the same feeling in one of Walther Flex's poems called "*Unrast*":

> *Mir ist, ich habe etwas geträumt,*
> *weiss nur nicht was—*
> *Mir ist, ich habe etwas versäumt,*
> *weiss nur nicht was—*
> *Mir ist, man wartet mein irgendwo,*
> *wüsst ich nur wer—*
> *Jetzt weiss ich's! Mein Herze, du wartest so,*
> *du bist so leer.*

How well I know this hollowed-out waiting for something—and everything to come bodes ill. I used to wait anxiously for mail from home to bring news of Father and Franz. But there has been no word from Father since the ill-fated *Volkssturm* training exercise that turned into battle, and Franz was last reported near Frankenstein, a small county seat near which Mama is buried in her native village. How well he knows from visits to relatives and bicycle outings the very territory which is now the front line! Now I am relieved when no mail comes—then nothing has changed; any change can only be for the worse.

Late next evening I am urgently summoned to the staff office. The leader on duty wants to clarify a garbled telephone message which has reached the camp in relays.

"How many brothers do you have?" she asks me.

"Only one now," I reply.

"Only one? Have you had word that he was wounded?"

"Yes, but he returned to active duty weeks ago."

"No, I mean since then. He was wounded a few days ago—a head wound."

Still composed, I demand to know: "Where is he hospitalized? I need to see him!"

"He was hospitalized till yesterday"—I hear the next words before she speaks—"and he will be buried tomorrow."

"No! Please, no!"

Outside night, wind, a fence obstructing my flight from a death I will not acknowledge. I need to keep running to shake myself free from a voice in my head shouting: Dead, Franz is dead! If only the night could swallow me into oblivion and become my grave, I would not have to listen to the terrible words. No, not Franzl! It isn't true! I love him too much to let him be dead!

I must wake up and the nightmare will be over. But every stumble tells me that I am awake and moving and alone in this night without dawn. A sliver of light from an insufficiently security-darkened window pierces my path and my senses. Light, people, talk, music—I shrink back into the dark and the moaning wind. Soon the lights will be out in the barracks, and the night will follow me in.

The wind flings the door out of my hand, making the accordion-player who sits in the dim glow of the heater miss a beat and look up in alarm. I leave the question in her glance unanswered and lie on my bunk, while she resumes her playing. On and on she plays, until her sentimental tunes drift into lullabyes, soothing me like Heia's hand when I was a little child.

Morning comes and a day like any other. In the evening we assemble for group singing. I slip into the last row to hide my silence. Every word has been an effort all day long, and now my lips refuse to open in song. The familiar tunes float past my ear, and now they sing a love song, sweet and sad, of soldiers gone to war and death—

> *. . . vielleicht deckt heut' schon manchen*
> *die kühle Erde zu,*
> *und einer*
> *war meiner—*
> *Gott geb' ihm die Ruh.*

My face is wet, and tears keep seeping from my eyes as the ocean of pain in my soul finds a release at last. I am empty and calm and infinitely weary, but I am no longer waiting.

No Taps

With the beginning of the Landeshut assignment only a few days away, I am granted an emergency leave at home, a short interruption on the trip in northeasterly direction. I arrive unannounced to find a refugee camp of women quartered in our apartment. Besides Mother and Annemie, the household has grown to include Aunt Gretl, with her two daughters and ancient mother-in-law, and another unrelated woman and her daughter and very young son. All of them have fled the provincial capital when the ring of Russian forces was about to close around the city of Breslau for a grueling siege of many weeks. The little boy, the only male among them, seems to whine most of the time.

At first my unexpected arrival seems to brighten the spirit of the women, as if being together might lend strength to each—an illusion that does not last. I learn that I am in time for my brother's funeral, which has been delayed by sheer fluke of circumstances. Wounded in the company post near Frankenstein, he had been transported to a hospital in a mountain resort not an hour's slow train ride from home. Did he realize that the train carried him through his hometown? Now he has returned to be buried among the dead of many wars in the garrison cemetery of Glatz. The thought of having him close in death is a small solace: no distant, lonely grave for him like so many others that lie untended from the time the earth is heaped upon them.

It seems incredible that the family had succeeded in wresting his body from the military machine for a private burial at home, a small miracle and an act of heroism. Exerting all of her powers of persuasion, Mother had pleaded with the hospital commandant to release the body to her, and he agreed to find a place on a hospital train through our town. But when the time came, it was little Annemie and our cousin Marianne who claimed him. Among the dead and dying stacked on stretchers, they searched the rows of wagons for the familiar face, walking through a nightmare of destroyed human beings. They found him, pale and handsome and unmarked by the tiny bit of metal that took his life.

Now he rests in a small building on the grounds of a school-turned-hospital that serves as a morgue. We stand huddled in a group, waiting for the soldiers to move the casket to a horse-drawn cortege. There is time to go in for a last look, and the others urge me to go with them. But I cannot endure to be close enough to touch the body that cannot feel my touch, to see the closed eyes that will never look on me with love again. My farewell to him was said before Christmas and will have to last into eternity.

Then the rites at the graveside are over, and handfuls of earth fall upon the lowered casket. I drop a few lumps in ritual obedience thinking:

"You cannot feel them, and nothing can hurt you any more. Wherever you may be, you are not in this wooden box; down there in the uniform lies nothing but a souvenir of your brief journey. The memories of the miles we traveled together are the real you, and they will never die."

In the days that follow I shun the company of the others who fluctuate between raving laments for the dead and indulging in glowing descriptions of all he was and all he could have been. Aunt Gretl is the most unrestrained and articulate in her grief. It pours forth unceasingly for the one we just buried, for her husband missing at sea, for all the men we all have lost, for her ruined home in Russian hands, and it mingles with woeful predictions for our future. Franz's death has stirred in her all the furies that have slumbered and are now unleashed at this moment of awakening.

"Why has God singled us out for such punishment? You see how much good all of your praying and running to church has done you, Hede [this to Mother]. He has taken, taken and, mind my words, He isn't done with us yet!"

Mother quietly weeps: "His will be done. He alone knows and will give us strength."

"We should have taken matters in our own hands and

hidden Franz. The war won't last much longer, and nobody would have been the wiser if he had turned up afterwards."

"You can't be serious. He may not have been a soldier by choice but he was no shirker," Annemie comes to his defense. "What do you think Father would have said or done to him if the thought had ever crossed Franz's mind!"

Against Aunt Gretl's onslaughts I build a barrier of stoic reticence to keep my own despair at bay. My refusal to wail and weep makes me a new target for her.

"I don't understand you at all, you of all people who I thought was so close to him. Are you an unfeeling monster that you can spare not one tear for your brother?"

"Not all the tears in the world will bring him back, and neither will all the noise you make change one thing of what is still ahead."

Although Aunt Gretl is only in her early forties, her dark hair is heavily streaked with gray now, and her ever mobile mouth that shared many a laugh with us in the past is drawn into a drooping line of suffering. Eyes ablaze in anger, she rages at anyone daring to contradict her.

"One of these days you will get your fill and learn to cry. You will end up worse than a beggar and run around with a Russian bastard in your swollen belly if you are lucky enough to live!"

I detest her coarseness. Mother interjects an embarrassed: "Gretl, Gretl!"

"Quit painting the devil on the wall. If everyone would see black on black as you do, we might as well give up now. It isn't over yet and until then there is still a chance that prophets of doom will have to eat their words," I counter in spite of my intention to stay out of her way. To keep my balance I must believe that the pain and dying and destruction have not been in vain.

"Stupid child, how little you know. All of your good grades in school mean nothing in the school of life."

In one of the dramatic mood swings that mark her personality she becomes sad and gentle.

"Poor girls, so young and so much heartache! Who would have thought that you would grow up in times such as these. Will you ever see good times again?"

Always her talk returns to Franz, "the most beautiful officer in Glatz" in her exaggerated vocabulary. I steel myself for yet another account of his last weeks at home of which I have no memory, the weeks after Christmas when the refugees from Breslau began living in our house.

"To think that Franz and Marianne would fall in love right under our very noses!"

"Mama, please let it be," pleads Marianne with brimming eyes.

"Child, we all know how you had eyes and ears only for each other, and you told me that you loved him."

"Don't you understand that I can't talk about it, Mother?" Marianne bursts crying from the room. I feel like running after her to commiserate with her for her mother's hurtful indiscretion, but the subject at stake is, for my own sake, too delicate to touch.

Until a few days ago I had no inkling of these developments, and these weeks that I jealously considered as stolen from me take on a new painful significance. My "cousin" and bosom friend Marianne and my brother—I have no right to feel hurt or betrayed because nothing has been taken from me and two people whom I love have been enriched. But I cannot rejoice and I do not even want to know about it.

Had she been toying with him and he fell for her? In our confidences Marianne had admitted to me how she exploited her magnetism on men for the delicious pleasure it gave her to fuel their desire and then retreat. As long as she practiced her witchcraft on strangers, I envied her skill but now I resent it. I, too, like to flirt, but playing with love is something I could never do and would not want to.

I am not even tempted to ask Marianne what Franz meant to her. What could she say? But the question plagues me: Would their love have lasted and would it have been as great if he were still alive?

I feel as isolated from her now as I do from the others.

Annemie and she are inseparable now after living like sisters for months. My life has nothing in common with them any more, or with this turbulent household, and leaving will be easy. Who knows, I may never be one of them again. When I go I mean to take the best clothes, keepsakes I treasure, and plenty of money, throw in some makeup and cigarettes for brighteners—anything can happen at any time, and I want to be ready to run. It is just as well that no ties remain.

The bleak days pass slowly and unhappily. Daily I visit Heia, more for her sake than mine, and I do not stay long because her tenderness has become a threat to my composure. At home Mother goes like a ghost about routine household chores, rarely speaking, and then only a few unconvincing words of encouragement, which her face belies, and of our Christian obligation to entrust our fate to God, and of hope that Father will still come home to us. She knows that his unit had been routed by the Russians; the men who came back reported that Father had gotten separated from them in his attempt to round up stragglers and been left behind in the head-over-heels escape. More we shall never learn.

"He should not have left you in the first place. Such a smart man in every other way," Aunt Gretl shakes her head in dismay.

"I couldn't hold him back any more than you could hold Leo," is Mother's lame reply.

"That is entirely different. Leo is much younger and was drafted. Josef, at his age and state of health, and one son already killed, had no need to go and no business going."

"He was doing his duty for the fatherland as he saw it," I break in, "if you can understand what that means. Let him— be." I almost said "rest in peace" because I know as surely as I am living that he, too, is dead, and I feel a guilty relief at the thought. More merciful for him not to have to face the death of his last son, the collapse of his family, and the bankruptcy of his staunch patriotism. Easier for me to be abandoned than to see my proud Father a broken man.

The rantings of one half-crazed woman and the pious resignation of the other become intolerable and drive me from the home that has become a madhouse. I flee to the grave on which the flowers are wilting and lean against the big old tree whose naked branches spread above it. When the wind rustles through the dry leaves underfoot, it seems that soothing murmurs reach my ear which form into words and voices. I feel engulfed in the presence of my dead brother and relive our last hour together. Once again we get ready for our last walk. His bandaged arm stands stiffly away from his body, and he cannot dress himself. I slide it carefully into the sleeve of his tunic, button it. When I kneel down in front of him to put his boots on, he pats my hair with his healthy hand. Ever so gently I slip the heavy field-gray coat over the wounded arm, then over the other, and close the stiff buttons slowly, delaying by moments our departure. Arm in arm we walk from the house. His injured arm excuses him from saluting. I carry my own bag so that his healthy arm can stay linked in mine. On and on we walk, never reaching the station and never saying the last farewell.

Alone in the night, I am assailed by desolation and thoughts of death. Tossing in tortured sleeplessness, I yearn to escape from my body to join him and the others where pain and despair are said to cease. The questions and predictions which Aunt Gretl has shouted in the light of day echo through the silence, and deep in my soul I know that much of what she said is true.

Last Stand

A high fence topped with barbed wire surrounds the munitions depot in a wooded area outside Landeshut. We live in low barracks hidden among the trees. Armed guards are posted at the exits and patrol the compound.

The *RAD* details serve daily by nailing lids on crates filled with cartridges; others sit at sewing machines securing small bags partially filled with premeasured quantities of powder. As far as we know, we are the only nonmilitary German personnel attached to the depot. It is administered by an army captain and his staff of officers and noncommissioned officers. Soldiers are in evidence everywhere in charge of foreign laborers and are occasionally seen accompanying small groups of Russian POWs in tattered uniforms. There is no mingling, except for the necessary communication on the top level of leadership. When dark descends, we are restricted to our barracks. Not the faintest glimmer of light betrays the existence of an installation or any human habitation near or far.

In the silence after lights-out, we listen for the ominous sound of planes, one in particular. Because of its peculiar engine noise nicknamed "Russian duck," it is said to be a low-flying reconnaissance plane. Miraculously, the "duck" fails to gather dangerous intelligence and never seems to risk a search during daytime. The nights remain undisturbed.

The strict order of daily activities is broken now and then by a few afternoon hours away from the depot, even an occasional weekend pass for girls with safe destination. Once my sister pays me a surprise visit. Pretty and cheerful as ever, she is like a flashback to another age. We walk in the woods beyond the camp, chatting of trivial things, enjoying the spring day. Only when leaving does she strike a serious note:

"Gina, see that you get home when the time comes."

Without these highly prized interruptions, the illusion of security might have been maintained indefinitely. They prove costly in terms of our morale.

The town where we seek a sense of freedom from the barbed-wire enclosure offers little distraction. But just walking in a normal small-town environment is a treat.

"Look at this!" The girls ahead of us have stopped at the entrance to the square. They are staring in consternation at a typed or printed sheet. Catching up, we all cluster around a list of names attached to a proclamation to the citizens of Landeshut which, in essence, reads:

"The enemy in our ranks threatens the security of your homeland and the success of our valiant armies. Under penalty of law you are hereby ordered to report to members of the field police any knowledge of deserters, and apprehend or detain them for local authorities. In case of resistance they are to be shot on sight. Desertion before the enemy is punishable by death, and complicity will be dealt with likewise. Be on the alert for these cowardly enemies of the people!"

As if hypnotized, we study the names that follow.

"It can't go on much longer if the soldiers are quitting," says one of the girls.

"That's what we thought weeks ago before we got here," replies another who has come with me from Czechoslovakia.

"Here is another one!"

I discover a somewhat shorter list of names on a telephone pole under the terse heading:

"Executed for cowardice and desertion."

Our stroll becomes a pilgrimage in search of these black lists. Any tree or pole or building is likely to display one.

We are to wage war against our own soldiers, these men who have fought and bled for six years and now desperately want to survive a lost cause—it has come to this! This "cause" Franz had termed an idea born of madness for which he would surely have to die. Father had silenced him with a stern warning that, away from home, such words would be called treason. But Franz served and died. Would he have run even now? No question about Father—

The thought of German soldiers deserting is still inconceivable to me, and yet, how often in camp have we toyed with the idea of daring an escape or simply not returning from an afternoon in town or a weekend pass. We are no different from the soldiers; they are as eager to live and rejoin their families at any price.

Troubled by ambivalent feelings, some of us seek out the local priest who has welcomed us to his home a few times before. In his quiet book-lined study we find no answers—there are no answers—but as always his personal calm and relaxed hospitality sooth the tensions. Although disdainful of Mother's weepy babbling about divine wisdom beyond our understanding, coming from him the same words kindle in me a minute measure of trust. He offers us books to take back to camp to while away the long evenings in confinement, thereby reassuring us that we will have a chance for another visit to return them.

Weekend passes are a mixed blessing. Many of the girls

come from areas already overrun by the Russians. They spend their weekends in gloomy inertia; others rail against fate and threaten desertion or suicide. Those who still go home and return whisper about signs of the approaching catastrophe and the fiery streaks they have seen in the eastern night sky.

On one weekend in Glatz, Mother hands me a bulky letter from Franz's commanding officer. An Iron Cross clatters on the table. The letter is written to a convalescent, with wishes for a speedy recovery and return to the unit. The field surgeon had assured the officer that Franz's wound was not dangerous, certainly not fatal. Mother is so listless and shrunken into herself that even a small matter like acknowledging the letter seems beyond her strength. Aunt Gretl, who never lacked energy enough for both of them, is an invalid, no longer able or inclined to help or torment anyone. Since Franz's funeral she has almost literally cried her eyes out and is struck by blindness which the doctor is not certain will reverse itself. I write the note in Mother's name and keep the letter and the Iron Cross to myself, an ironic postscript to my gentle brother's life.

Official news and rumors breed barely contained hysteria in camp. Even ancient prophecies surface in hushed conversations, adding to the feeling of gloom. Days after Hitler's proclamation that "Berlin is German! Berlin will remain German!" the capital is a battlefield. Toward the end of April, 1945, we hear that Göring has withdrawn for health reasons from his duties as *Reichsmarschall*. I can no longer condemn any ordinary citizen, let alone any soldier, who deserts the lost cause for which he was ordered to fight. But when a prominent member of the government dodges the last consequences of situations which he himself helped to bring about, then he is nothing but a miserable coward. *Der Führer* and Goebbels are said to be engaged in battle in the ruins of Berlin. Is this a last attempt to rally through personal example all remaining forces or is it camouflaged suicide?

There is wildly optimistic talk that the Western Allies have accepted a truce and are regrouping with German forces in the west to reverse the Russian advance. The truth, according to a secretly overheard foreign newscast, is quite different: Himmler has offered to the Western Allies unconditional surrender but because Russia was excluded, the offer has been rejected. Nothing is what it seems, everything is ambiguous. Because of the millions of victims we should keep hating and thirsting for revenge, and yet everyone seems to be waiting for the end of the senseless slaughter and for peace at any price. What has become of our once so proud and beautiful fatherland?

By now the Russian offensive has rolled halfway across Germany to the north of us, leaving the camp caught in a pocket edged by the fiercest fighting. The girls from Saxony realize that they may never see their families again. A few, in desperation, make good their escape from camp. After that, all passes and permissions for visits in town are canceled.

We have been issued gas masks and instructed to carry them with us everywhere outside the barracks. What is going to happen? *Der Führer* has been quoted as saying to a highly decorated officer:

"May God forgive me the last four days of war!"

What has he meant by this?

The rainy morning of May 2, 1945, is perfectly suited as the backdrop for more disastrous news: *Der Führer* has died in the battle of the *Reichskanzlei*; at least, that is the official version. When the monotonous pounding of the rain stops intermittently, the silence outside is spooky. At first the officers were walking around as if stupefied and then assembled for a top-level conference. Our camp leader, who usually turns up anywhere and everywhere unexpectedly, has become all but invisible, and the few who have seen her comment that her face is ashen and her eyes swollen from weeping.

Dönitz, the new commander-in-chief, apparently has decided to discontinue the battle against the Western powers in order to concentrate the remnants of the *Wehrmacht* against the Russians. Instead of victory and reconstruction, the most he hopes to secure for the German people is "a bearable existence."

The tragic turn of events has left me unshaken as if they were happening somewhere else to another person, while some of the girls are breaking down with grief and fear.

Nothing that has happened, or can happen yet, will match the desolation I have already experienced. But I am glad that I am not at home just now to hear the hysterical tirades that Aunt Gretl is even now bound to launch against a man who was larger than life, for better or worse, who made our country strong and proud and who sacrificed himself and all of us for his grandiose plans. Before I condemn him, I need time to sort out my feelings. Neither can I suddenly rejoice at the tenacious rumor that the Western Allies have accepted the German surrender after all and will side with us against the Russians. The turnabout is like treason. A few weeks ago the slogan still was *Wir kapitulieren nie* ("We will never surrender") and now, unconditionally, and we are ready to welcome our enemies as saviors from the Russian terror. Such simplistic notions do not consider that the Americans will have many an axe to grind with all kinds of party functionaries and armies that fought against them. Why should they suddenly embrace them as comrades?

Rumors that affect us immediately make a lot more sense. The townspeople of Landeshut are said to have been alerted for evacuation. A breakthrough is expected from the north to unite the northern and southern Russian flanks and cut off the valiantly resisting Silesian front lines. Work in the depot is called off. We are ordered to pack, certain of imminent dismissal. The day passes in tension and near panic.

In the evening two officers join a camp assembly to discuss the military situation, reassuring us that discharge proceedings have been started and that we will surely be able to reach our destinations. Relieved and almost happy we go to bed.

Next morning, May 7, 1945, the first names are called to report to the staff office for discharge. Almost simultaneously the depot commandant issues an order to report to work immediately. He has frozen all discharges because the dismissal of foreign civilians in recent days has reduced the manpower to a barely operational level. Our leaders appeal to us to be reasonable and obey—the disbanding of a sister camp on the previous day is explained away as a regrettable, premature action.

We walk slowly in the direction of the depot, but by some common initiative gather along the way and pass it by, and march to the headquarters building in force. The commandant awaits us on the steps, hand on his holster:

"What is this? Mutiny? You were ordered to your places of work. Let this serve as your warning: I will not tolerate mutiny under my command. Furthermore, I have given orders to shoot anyone foolish enough to attempt to break from this compound and I will not hesitate personally to down one or more of you. Until further notice you will fulfill your duties as usual or suffer the consequences for insubordination."

The spontaneous, unorganized protest fizzles before this threat of violence. A man like Ribbentrop can defect unscathed but a group of harmless, helpless girls who want to run for their lives remains imprisoned at gunpoint. What heroics has the commandant in mind? Our armies are in a state of total dissolution; all that is left of a *Führerhauptquartier* and *Oberkommando der Wehrmacht* is the humbly named *Oberkommando der deutschen Truppen*. The party and all of its organizations have ceased to function. We must be the last, the very last, *RAD*-unit in existence owing only to the irrational whim of a fanatical officer.

But within hours the decision is reversed. Among the first I exchange my uniform for a breezy spring dress and, discharge papers duly signed in my pocket, race to the station. Miraculously, trains are still running. Mine is next to the last to leave Landeshut.

Homecoming

The sign on the long building, which is flanked on either side by platforms, tracks, more platforms, other tracks in broad profusion, reads *Glatz Hauptbahnhof*. Always a busy station at which even the fast long-distance trains stop and freight traffic seldom ceases, on this day it resembles a railroad graveyard. Trains are still arriving but few are leaving. Unloaded they crawl toward the switching yard, then on to dead tracks where they rumble to a halt and stand abandoned.

In and around the station building reigns bedlam. The platforms are a congested scene of feverish movement and motionless islands, people swarming everywhere in opposite directions, stumbling over and around others lounging in exhausted stupor between mountains of baggage. Soldiers fully armed, with huge field packs on their backs; civilians, young and old; the wounded in soiled bandages; steel-helmeted field police; nurses; women volunteers with trays of coffee—they are the combined casts of all the wartime drama that has unfolded in this setting over the past six years. Now they are flung together for the last tragic scene of the last act for which no script has been written.

I dive into the jostling mass of bodies and baggage toward the exit without pausing to check on a passenger connection into town. My role in the drama calls for another scene in another setting, which turns out to be a replay in miniature of the spectacle I left behind at the station.

At home I find the hallway stacked with suitcases and bundles. Mother, Annemie, and the resident refugees are still packing, adding, discarding, searching for some important article. Making my way through the hall, I stupidly ask what they are doing.

"Getting ready."

"Ready for what?"

"To leave."

"Where, for heaven's sake?"

No answer.

An officer of our acquaintance who is on garrison duty because of a stiff leg stops by in the evening. No longer afraid of tuning to a foreign station, we find BBC and wait for the news. Silently we cling to every word of the broadcast that announces the cessation of hostilities at midnight, May 8—tomorrow night.

"Well, folks, now you have heard it: The war is over!" proclaims the lieutenant to break the tension.

"What now?" someone asks.

"I will peel off my uniform—without regrets, I might add—and trust that the Russians won't be interested in a cripple like me."

"Six years of blood and tears for nothing," sighs Mother.

"And all because of that scoundrel who thought he was God Almighty and wanted to rule the world!" With her eyesight Aunt Gretl is recovering her personality.

"I think we must let history judge him, permit me to say. One man alone could not have accomplished what he did nor cause this utter disaster. You know that I never was a fan of his but I reserve judgment," he corrects her politely.

"Amen to this," I think knowing that the topic will come up over and over again and not as easily be put to rest.

"I wonder what peace is really like," muses Annemie. "I was nine years old when all of this started." At fifteen she is a young woman much more polished and confident than I and often taken for my older sister.

"It may be awhile before you find out, little one," I try to tease her. "They say that peace is breaking out, and that sounds as bad as war to me. But what have we to lose," I add morosely, wishing I could take back the words that bring back the terrible feeling of loss, but I really feel that little matters what happens now.

"If only Daddy were home," from Aunt Gretl's little girl.

"Couldn't you stay with us?" Marianne asks the lieutenant.

"I wish I could, but my mother and sister wouldn't like that at all. Seriously, in times like these families belong together, and you are fortunate to have each other. You will find strength in each other. There is little a man could offer you now, except a strong back, but no protection."

Long after midnight after listening to another newscast, he takes his leave.

"*Auf Wiedersehen*, and God be with us all."

Last Day of War

Harsh awakening to a cacophony at dawn. The window panes ring with the vibrations of sound closeby. Clatter of wagon wheels, motors roaring, sharp cracks of rifle fire, and the drum roll of not-so-distant artillery—a doomsday orchestra is tuning up for its grande finale.

We must find out what is happening outside. From the gate we can see a main road a block away. *Gott sei Dank*, the Russians haven't come! German troops and German vehicles fill the road curb to curb, and the field-gray stream keeps flowing around the bend in orderly formations. We edge closer to stand among other civilians who seem to form a reception line for our returning soldiers.

"Where are you coming from?" someone asks.

"From Wartha. Now Holy Mary will have to look after her town by herself," says a soldier in passing, referring to a shrine of the Virgin, a place of pilgrimage.

"Are you the last ones?"

"No, there are more in the mountains holding the pass."

The artillery must be the sound of battle for the pass, a mere ten kilometers away from here.

"Still ten kilometers to go! Just think, the Russians haven't gained any more than that in almost two months," I remark hopefully to Marianne. Frankenstein, where Franz was wounded in March, is about twenty kilometers away.

"Then what do you think the rifle shots mean that are much closer?"

"I don't know—unless someone has decided to end it all or," I add with a shudder, "some deserters have been caught." And I recall the posters with names in Landeshut which are bound to be here and everywhere else as well.

"Surely not that! It will be over in a few hours anyway."

Mother orders us home. "Let's stay together. We must decide what to do."

"The first thing I must do is to report back for a residence permit and ration cards. The offices should be open by the time I get there," I tell her and start looking for a break among the marchers.

"Be careful and hurry home," she pleads.

"There is still time as long as they keep marching like this." Indeed, the disciplined formations do not look like a head-over-heels retreat. But how many others will be sacrificed to buy time for the troops we now see?

The offices in the city hall are deserted, only a few old men stand idly in the hallway, looking askance at my search for service. But discipline and the habit of years die hard, and I ask one of them:

"Where should I report?"

"Who knows where," he shrugs. "You'd better go home."

I feel an utter fool to have expected everything to go on as before and suddenly realize that not only the time-honored German bureaucracy is breaking down but all law and order as I know them. From the edge of this abyss I run to Heia, who has never failed me.

"Thank God, you made it back. That is the main thing!"

"What do you think will happen now?"

"I wish I could tell you. We are staying. And you?"

I don't know but for the moment I am glad to be with her.

"First of all let's do something about the ration cards you couldn't get. That much we can do for you," and she and her kind-hearted employer wrap a package of durable marching provision in case the family decides to run. Now at least, no one at home will have to share supplies with me.

"I don't like to see you go, but they'll worry at home if you stay any longer." With that, Heia makes the sign of the cross on my forehead as always when one of us children left on a journey. She is probably watching from the window after I leave, but I won't turn around to see her cry.

Home again, questions, indecision. The door bell rings. Like an apparition from the past, a tall, remarkably handsome officer salutes.

"My name is Wolf. We were passing a street sign that I recognized as Franz's address, so I quickly fell out to ask about my friend."

Stunned by the news of Franz's death, he identifies himself as the field surgeon who diagnosed the wound as not serious.

"He should not have died," he says. "But some such cases take unexpected turns," he adds, the physician conquering the friend.

"*Herr Doktor*, I know you must go," Mother reaches out as if to hold him back. "Please tell us what we should do."

"With four young girls? Leave the city and waste no time," he says and is gone. At last a decisive word! The advice of a stranger—perhaps a message from Franz?

We lose no time in carrying the most indispensable baggage downstairs, loading it on bicycles and on our backs, and leave town on paths only the natives know to avoid the congested main roads, where gaps between military units are filling up with fleeing civilians, drifting wherever the stream will carry them. Pushing the awkward bicycles, the caravan of two women, four teenage girls, and the ancient grandmother makes slow progress. Our destination for the time being is the native village of Mother and Aunt Gretl, a mere eight kilometers away, where their brother's wife keeps the farm and country inn going with the help of an old Polish maid-servant and, until recently, a Ukranian field hand.

We labor up the steep hill at the edge of town where the street meets the highway, and look aghast at the spectacle before us: Here, too, an endless mass of soldiers, horse-drawn wagons with household goods, women doubled up under heavy burdens, a few military trucks grinding in low gear. We melt into the sad procession which gathers more stragglers like us as it slowly moves away from town. Where are all these people bound? West, to the Americans; into the woods and mountains to hide; anywhere to find a place to rest; anywhere at all, just away from the Russians! Everybody talks to everyone, but the same words are repeated over and over: where?—home was—come along—still time—what do you think?—how long until?

Between us we toss about the possibilities of living and dying, and any one of them may be the wrong choice: Should we turn back home after all and wait? Should we make up our minds to stay in the village that beckons under the sparkling, flawless sky? Or would we stand a better chance choosing the gypsy life on the road west? The roadside is cluttered with bundles whose value has been outstripped by the compulsion to keep moving toward the illusive grand prize, Life. Soon we would be too tired and leave ours in the ditch, too. The longest eight kilometers we ever walked convince us of the foolishness of trying to escape. We break out of the column and enter the shelter of Mother's old home.

But within hours restlessness grips us and drives us back into the thick of the desperate migration. We have left so much behind in town which we could now hide under the rafters of the old house, in the barn, beneath the trapdoor to the dark cellar. Eight kilometers back to town in less than half the time, unloaded. A friend we meet looks at us in alarm, tells Mother to get the girls away quickly before the victorious hordes arrive—the celebration in town is bound to be a carnage! Another grueling eight-kilometer trek with loaded bicycles.

By nightfall, the public room of the inn is a refugee camp. Our two rooms upstairs seem like a luxurious haven compared to the helter-skelter of bodies and baggage below. Exhaustion overtakes us, blotting out today and thoughts of tomorrow.

4

Life among the Victors and the Vanquished

Inn at the Crossroads

At the entrance to the village stands the manor house, shaded by century-old trees and hidden by a row of tall bushes that spill over the rock wall. The highway slopes in a leisurely curve to the valley and straightens on level ground to reveal a view of the Biele River and the twin road on its other bank. Farm houses with little garden strips, bushes, and white picket fences border the road at irregular intervals, crowding closer together in the center of the village where the road divides at a narrowly angled delta. One arm runs in a straight line between meadows and fields on one side and an unbroken row of houses opposite, facing the mountain range that lifts the fields gently toward the edge of the woods. The other arm of the road veers sharply right toward the bridge across the river and just beyond it meets its twin at the stone steps to the cemetery hill, which is crowned by an old whitewashed church. It traces the cemetery wall and drops over the hill, reappearing as a silver ribbon on its way to the mountains, and is lost out of sight in the rising woods.

The inn squats in the widest part of the delta, flanked by the divided road. A fenced flower garden borders on the connecting link between the roads, and back from this lane, hard at the curve toward the bridge, stands a taller, box-shaped building, the Iron Cross, which comes closest to being a hotel in this rural community.

The inn faces toward the river and the church. Its front gable is wreathed by the branches of a huge chestnut tree by the door. On a concrete strip next to the entrance stands a single gasoline pump, witness to the enterprising spirit of the innkeeper in better times and his love for motor vehicles. On the narrowing part of the property lies the farmyard with a water pump in its center and a tall barn, joined at right angles to a two-story apartment house, once intended as the retirement home for the old innkeeper. First and foremost a farm, the place has proliferated into this conglomeration of structures and purposes to take advantage of its unique location between the roads.

In summer the old stone house is always cool behind its thick walls, and snug and cozy against the winter winds. There are weeks when the public room with the bar and half a dozen tables is deserted, except for one tucked behind the tile stove where the regulars meet for card games and beer. The private dining room next to the barroom is as much a part of the family living quarters as it is for the use of the guests.

The center of all activity is the kitchen beyond it, with its broad coal cooking stove and large table, set in front of a long wooden bench between windows that look out on the flower garden. From the kitchen, a door leads to a small vestibule toward the garden exit, another to the barroom, one out into the flag-stoned hall behind the barroom, and a fourth, up a few steps, to the master bedroom. Under the same roof beyond the hall is the stable for the cattle. The summer boarders from the city, who used to stay in upstairs rooms, would go to sleep to the languid sounds of cows stirring on their beds of straw, mooing softly, and awaken in the morning to the clatter of milking utensils.

Now two upstairs rooms at the corner toward the bridge, which open from a small common vestibule, have become our refuge. The room directly above the entrance, its single window shielded by the chestnut tree, is nicknamed *Lazarett* ("hospital") because several beds stand side by side with narrow aisles between them. A wardrobe, washstand, bookcase, dresser, and a table with chairs in front of the window complete the furnishings. The other, larger, room is crowded with upholstered furniture—some of which doubles as beds—a utility cabinet of undefinable origin and purpose, and two enormous wardrobes. The toilets, primitive by city standards, are downstairs.

When we move into these quarters on the last night of the war, the ground floor is still teeming with the transients who have crowded in for a respite on their uncertain trek. Upstairs behind closed doors we cannot hear them. The frenzied activity on the roads has lost its momentum and the noise has subsided. The last sounds we hear through the open window are the mountain stream splashing over the rocks and the breeze murmuring in the chestnut tree.

A Day in May

The brilliantly shining morning steeps the earth. The air, simple and pure save for the fragrance of lilacs, seems more than impersonal nature—seems somehow to respond to the affection of the reaching sun. It is, indeed, one of those times when earth never seemed more fair, when each young blade of grass and each bud and the song of each lark above betokens some kind fresh beginning. It is a time—a rare time—when the soul in harmony with nature yearns like the lark to spread its wings and soar away from the reality of human tragedy. Oblivious to the dark deeds of men who violate the earth and each other, nature has put on its finery once again, following its own eternal laws in an abiding cycle of life.

On this day made for happiness the village waits in

deathlike silence. More populated than during its most lucra-
tive tourist seasons, it nonetheless seems deserted.

We have gotten dressed in a hurry, stirred by Mia's excited wake-up call:

"Hannsdorf is burning! There is shooting in Glatz! The
Russians will be here any minute!"

Shortly after midnight, when the German troops had to
surrender in the mountain pass, the first Russian units have
rolled into Glatz. My lovely hometown would remain untouched if the end of war really meant peace!

At the open windows we stand and listen. Finally the
birdsong is drowned out by the drone of motors approaching. Trucks packed with soldiers in olive uniforms roar into
and through the village, no one noticing that some vehicles
have left the column until the farmyard rings with shouts,
sharp and loud like commands. The scene is one of military
order. Within moments the door to the Iron Cross next door
flies open, and a field-gray line slowly files through it and
stands bordering the alley. The enemies of four bloody years
salute each other. The Russians hand out cigarettes to the dis-
armed German soldiers and march them out of sight. There is
no blood bath, no execution on the spot, no screaming—just
a calm, orderly take-over. And the trucks keep roaring by, intermittently spilling their human cargo around the pump in
the farmyard. The rumored violence and retribution surely
belong only to a war that ended last night.

Gradually a few civilians venture out to witness the his-
toric spectacle. We go downstairs to the kitchen for breakfast
but more than that, to talk and plan what to do next.

"This isn't at all what I expected. You all saw how decent
the Russians behaved toward our soldiers. We have probably
worried unnecessarily," I am inviting confirmation of my
hopes.

"But these are only the first ones, and they are in a hurry
to keep going," cautions Mother.

"We could have stayed in your comfortable apartment
instead of fighting the crowds yesterday and wearing ourselves out pushing bicycles back and forth." Hindsight is one

of Aunt Gretl's specialties. This time she is playing into my hand.

"What are we doing here then?" I press my optimistic assessment of the situation, and Aunt Gretl picks up on the thought:

"Why wouldn't we be as safe in Glatz as here? Besides, we could look after the apartment; abandoned, it is more likely to be looted."

"Do as you please," says Mia. "I will try to keep the rooms for you in any case."

Between our watching what is going on outside and our weighing the pros and cons of our next step, morning drifts into afternoon. We decide to return to Glatz, leaving all but the most essential baggage behind.

Ignored by the passing troops, we walk on the shoulder of the highway and reach the edge of town. In passing, we ask other civilians about conditions in Glatz, and no two answers are the same. On the outskirts the streets are ominously empty. Then there are Russian soldiers loitering aimlessly, brazenly eyeing us girls, grinning, calling to us. Oh, to be back in the village!

A soldier jostles Aunt Gretl, grabbing her hand bag. Flailing her free arm and shouting outrage, she fights for her bag. The soldier draws back, laughing. We pass store windows, splintered and gaping. Raucous singing pours from a tavern. On a strip of grass below the embankment at the railroad overpass, we halt almost involuntarily. A makeshift wooden cross, crowned by a steel helmet, rises on a fresh grave. To think that someone had to die here in the last moments of war, to think that someone—comrade or stranger—spared the time to honor him with a burial! We gaze silently at the humble, temporary monument. Not the most elaborate wreath placed by a head of state at a gigantic memorial to the Unknown Soldier, whom friend and foe revere, can equal the blossoming weeds scattered on this mound in simple, heartfelt compassion.

Every block stretches interminably. Every soldier is seen as a threat. At last at our house, all is quiet and no one about.

To Lose a War

On the first landing we pause to read the note at a neighbor's door:

"Please do not enter this apartment. My wife has taken her life." But the door stands ajar.

"Do you think she is in there?" someone whispers.

Aunt Gretl has crossed the hall and motions us to follow:

"We must respect her death. She has lived and died according to her convictions."

Dignified as in life, fully dressed, with the party badge in her lapel, lies this proud woman on a couch.

We climb the stairs, horror-stricken, find our apartment untouched, and collapse from tension and relief.

Someone in passing tells us that the grocer around the corner is dividing up his remaining stock. Food—none of us had given a thought to it! Marianne and I set out to investigate. At the street corner a knot of foreign civilians parts in mock deference, heels click, arms fly up in the Nazi salute:

"*Heil* Hitler!"

We force ourselves to walk on calmly. Almost too late we arrive at the store and feel lucky to garner some flour, sugar, and grits. Again past the smirking foreigners and the apartment that is a morgue, we reach home with a fearful inkling of what lies in store for us.

In succeeding hours, hues of nightmare overshadow the reality of earth reborn, and gone are the illusions of peace that fleetingly touched our hearts in the earlier hours of the day. Far away the sun setting in self-indulgent splendor seems a divine mockery of our distress. The approaching darkness fills us with dread of forces blacker than the spring night closing in.

Lilacs in Bloom

A frame of wood and metal, a mattress, a fluffy pillow, and a soft coverlet—no place is more comforting than the familiar bed. It encloses the body to which it has become accustomed in countless nights, flowing about it unobtrusively, being there without being felt, giving back the warmth given. Without a life of its own, it sensually caresses the limbs that stretch and shift, always yielding, gently conforming. I luxuriate in the touch of the soft cocoon, feeling cuddled, safe, inaccessible. The mellow dark becomes another wrap, an insulation against the harsh life and light of day. To lie here, curled up and quiet forever, without conscious thought or desire, to drift into oblivion, and never to fear and fight and live, not even dream . . . . Sleep cheats me of indulging longer in the pleasurable sensation of being at home in my own bed and strangely content.

In the morning I rise in wide-awake apprehension of whatever might befall, hastily smooth the covers as always, fluff the pillow, returning the night's source of solace to its utilitarian insensibility.

The premonition of the previous evening springs to life with the rattling of the door. Instinctively, we girls slip into the kitchen, the least likely place to attract unwanted callers and plunderers. We marvel at the calm voices of our mothers who answer the door. They treat the intruders like guests, never betraying by word or tone of voice what they feel and fear. Single or in pairs, these seem uncertain of their reason for entering the apartment, open drawers and cabinets, lift the bedding, as if taking stock. Grandfather's gold watch is the only item one of them takes. Even Franz's dress uniform and his riding boots, polished to a mirror shine, remain in a wardrobe undisturbed. Between visits, Mother and Aunt Gretl drop on kitchen chairs, shaking from relief and in anticipation of the next banging at the door that may not prove as harmless.

Mother suddenly remembers the pistol in Father's locked desk drawer. The discovery of a weapon in the house would equal a death sentence.

"My God, we are done for!"

"If we get rid of it they won't find it," states Aunt Gretl, who has regained her old resoluteness in the face of danger.

We have a weapon, a treasure, and all they can see is danger!

"Give me the desk key. I want that pistol."

Mother looks at me aghast without making a move to get the key. Aunt Gretl charges at me as if to strike:

"Do you want to get all of us killed? You are insane!"

I never felt saner or calmer. "You don't understand. I don't mean to use it on myself or anybody else, at least not now. But I want a way out if it becomes necessary."

"You are a threat to all of us. Over my dead body will you lay hand on that pistol."

Short of a physical struggle against the two women, I don't have a chance to get my way. Mother hands the key to her sister who takes the pistol gingerly and hides it in her apron. She walks downstairs unhurriedly and through the garden to the edge of the canal. No one stops the middle-aged woman on her morning stroll, and she makes sure that no one sees or hears the splash when she tosses the weapon into the water.

There is no escape for me now. Many others did not throw their chances away. The woman in the apartment below ours, the doctor who after a lifetime of saving lives took his family with him into death away from shame and despair, among them my pretty classmate with the largest, saddest, dark eyes I had ever seen on anyone. They had a choice and chose. Deprived of my right to choose life or death, I am resentful of Aunt Gretl, who took it from me.

The neighborhood comes alive with frantic activity. Two blocks of residences are systematically being cleared for military quarters. It is only a matter of time before our turn will come; the callers of the morning must have been official inspectors, assessing space and accommodations. Better to leave voluntarily before the hordes arrive! The village and the inn filled with refugees seem years and miles away, too distant to return to under present conditions. We think of Father's friend in whose large villa at the edge of town or in the buildings of his adjoining factory we will surely find refuge.

He looks at us with sympathy and alarm. Eight Russian

officers reside in the villa; he and his wife and secretary are confined to a small office at the back of the house.

"I can't turn you away. But the only place I can offer you is the workers' lunchroom. And you won't be the only ones there."

A narrow, blackened staircase leads from the yard behind the villa to a dingy room with a few tables and benches. There is scarcely room to sit among the women and children who already occupy it. When my eyes get used to the semi-darkness after the brilliant sunshine outside, I recognize a former classmate, an unusually delicate girl, a pampered only child, with her widowed mother whose professor-husband fell into disgrace along with the Brüning regime between the wars. We hardly exchange a word, reluctant to acknowledge a meeting in these circumstances.

Somehow everybody finds a place, sitting or lying down to rest that night. It takes but little space for the weary to shut themselves into their own isolation and to sleep, or feign sleep to keep from disturbing those next to them. Silence is an unwritten, unspoken rule lest we betray our presence.

Mother follows her instincts to provide food for us. Ignoring her personal safety, she ventures into the villa to spend hours in the kitchen with Russian orderlies and cooks who accept her help, unquestioning. Somehow she smuggles some of their food into the hideout. When she arrives, we know that everyone in the villa is busy feasting and not likely to roam on the grounds. It is for us girls the one chance to leave our prison unseen. We slip around to the back of the building and breathe the fresh air hungrily, drinking in the warmth of the incredibly bright sunshine; each day seems to surpass the other in springtime glory. A lilac bush overflows with blossoms and scent, a lone messenger of spring and life and nature's everlasting, insensitive continuum. We break a branch to remember that life beyond the dark room goes on relentlessly, and to remember the joys of other springs that have been.

The nights become unbearably long; without any physical exertion by day, sleep refuses to come. I yearn for sleep, be it temporary or eternal. Death is becoming a friend; the enemy has a new name now: Rape. The residue of many catechism classes, throughout which the SIXTH COMMANDMENT was pronounced with the emphasis of capital letters, and the influence of an old-maid stepmother, who was scandalized even by the mention of a kiss, have stamped for me the label "sin" on every sexual thought and hidden even the most natural desire behind a still closed door. Vaguely aware of what I and others brought up in exaggerated protectiveness considered the ultimate offense against God, we fear rape as the ultimate crime and shame. And the reports and rumors that have preceded the Russians imply that any German woman is to them free for the taking. Unreasonable fear of rape rises in every woman's heart at the sight of every Russian.

Bumbling steps make the stairs creak; hands tap against the wooden wall. I stiffen with fear that they might find the latch on the dark door. Alertness as much as fear, because since the pistol sank in the water of the canal, I keep my pocket knife on me or within reach at all times. If the fumbling hands should find the latch, I am ready to cut the vein to spill my life in a red spurt of defiance and undefiled dignity. The drunken steps recede, and the dark moment passes, fading slowly into the light of another sparkling morning. The blue lilac blossoms on the table still spread their fragrance unashamedly, insistently: You are young, you are alive; leave the irreversible act undone until there is no other way! Live!

Mother knows that our hideout is no longer secret; the open highway to the village is a lesser risk than any place in town where stories of violence become more commonplace every day. The elite troops, proud and disciplined, who surged through the village on the first day, were the exception, not the norm. We must get away to where the near woods, if nothing else, would promise temporary safety. Above all, we must get away from the nights in the proximity of drunken celebrants.

At a mealtime before dark, we leave town to avoid the menace of another night in our dark prison. The highway is deserted and gloriously free, and for no reason at all we think of funny things to say and laugh. With nerves stretched to a breaking point, laughing and crying are just a chord away from each other.

On the Farm

Mia, the mistress of the farm and inn, receives us with mixed feelings. The stream of refugees that flowed through the public rooms has dwindled to an intermittent trickle, these homeless drifting on after a short rest to where they might find a more permanent refuge, or reversing their flight to where home used to be. Once again alone with her children—a cherubic, blue-eyed daughter of four and a chubby baby boy—and an elderly aunt who looks after the children, she welcomes the influx of our family group as if, indeed, there were safety in numbers when Russians pull into the yard, reducing the odds of individual danger. But the business woman, the manager that she is, at once grasps the liability of having seven more at table for who knows how long.

Already in town an order has been issued for all sixteen- to thirty-year-olds to register for labor. Taking her cue, she anticipates a similar order in the village and intends to claim us as workers in her establishment. Somewhat uncomfortably I remember the old innkeeper, now deceased, and one of his standing jokes. When during our family's Sunday visits the coffee would be steaming in mugs around platters of cake on the table, he would announce with a twinkle:

"He who does not work shall not eat."

I never liked the seemingly ungracious invitation and just once wanted to take him at his word. But in the face of such country bounty after scarce city weeks I never had the fortitude. No longer in jest, his dictum is now dead serious law in his daughter-in-law's house.

Divided among so many hands, the work in house and out overburdens no one, but its schedule depends on the unpredictable presence of Russians. When the traffic through

the village increases periodically but the house remains undisturbed, the women continue working downstairs but the
girls are exiled upstairs. Most often we read, but sometimes
we idle away the hours, trying to get our finger nails in shape
after working in the fields or doing our hair.

"*Ufftockan, auftakeln*, that's all you have on your
mind," laughs Annemie, mimicking Mia's disapproval of our
city ways.

"Just because we lost the war doesn't mean that we have
to be ugly hags. Let her talk," comments Marianne calmly,
continuing to put rollers in her hair.

"What I wouldn't give for a real bath in a tub instead of
Katzenwäsche in this little puddle," I sigh. "If I can't be beautiful, at least I would like to be clean."

Without running water upstairs, daily ablutions are at a
minimum, especially when we don't dare go for water to the
kitchen or to the pump in the yard. We have to take turns
washing in a small enamel basin that is refilled from a pitcher
and emptied into a bucket. Worst of all are the times when we
are cut off from the toilets and have to use the bucket for
other purposes.

"*Zustände wie bei den alten Germanen*," we observe in
lighter moods, but usually the perpetrator becomes the target
for snide remarks and furious glances.

Marianne's golden locks form a halo around her face
when we are allowed to reappear downstairs. She won't get
away with it.

"For whom have you dolled yourself up again?" is Mia's
sarcastic welcome. "Gretl, if she doesn't have better sense,
you ought to explain to your daughter what she is asking
for."

Reluctant to chastise her pride and joy, Aunt Gretl nevertheless has to agree that the prettier a girl the more likely she
is to attract attention.

"All of you girls will do yourselves and us a favor if you
are as inconspicuous as possible. Don't leave your scarves
and aprons upstairs any more—I think you should wear
them from now on whenever you come downstairs or go out-

side. We don't always have advance warning of surprise company."

We hate our disguises as "Russian-spooks." Mother has found long wrap-around aprons and head scarves for us to wear so that we are covered head to toe, with only the face showing. They are supposed to make us look dreadfully old and uninviting to anyone with immoral designs, and we feel ugly enough in them to dislike ourselves. But anything is better than to attract the attention of a Russian.

As the oldest and strongest of the girls, I must share some of the chores of the old servant woman, who is surly but an indefatigable worker. When dawn touches the night sky with the first tinge of day, the oxcart clatters from the yard across the bridge, past the church, across the railroad, and over rutted paths to the outlying fields. There the old woman swings the scythe rhythmically, felling the tender clover and grass, while I fork the cut feed onto the cart. The dew moistens our bare legs with a delicious chill, and when the first rays of the sun pierce the woods beyond, the field is turned into a glittering expanse of diamonds on green cloth. From afar cocks signal the beginning of a new day, and nearby the swish of the scythe accompanies the trill and twitter of birds readying for flight. I feel alive in the freshness of this morning solitude, conscious of the timelessness of primitive chores, while perspiration trickles over my face like dew and muscles strain with every lifting of the fork. Now and then the old woman urges the ox to move the cart closer, lavishing on him more words and more feeling than on any fellow human.

The cart loaded, we trudge back to the village to the inn where the animals stir restlessly in the stable. In the dank, warm semidarkness we work among the cows, throwing the old straw from the stalls into a wheelbarrow and putting down clean, dry sheaves, then emptying the load on the dung heap at the back of the house where it settles, steaming, on the residue of previous stable cleanings. When the troughs are filled with water and the cows have the freshly cut feed before them, I can go upstairs for my morning toilet and, if all are still asleep, for a half-awake doze among the sleepers.

Once the day has begun for everybody, there is little silence or solitude. When no Russian soldiers are about, people drift in and out, calling for their customary jugs of milk; neighbors stop in with tales they have heard from someone who knows an unnamed source with access to a radio. Radios have become a rarity, are either securely hidden or long departed with passing Russians. Mail and newspapers no longer exist, but rumors flourish.

Mia and her favorite neighbor exchange the newest gossip whenever that woman of whom I think as the mean tongue comes for milk in the mornings. Because we detest the woman and her influence on Mia, Marianne and I punctuate her remarks with asides to each other in English. Hearing words she cannot understand irritates her, and we know it.

"Are you girls studying Russian?" she wants to know.

"No, we are keeping up our English so we can translate for you when the Americans come," says Marianne, picking up on a rumor and teasing her at the same time.

"English won't do you a bit of good when the Czechs take over. You ought to learn something from your Aunt Mia instead." So now the Czechs will be our next plague according to the latest rumors, and she always knows the latest.

"Well, we will need English in any case when we go back to school. We might as well practice until that time comes."

I should have known better than to make such a comment. The woman cackles delightedly:

"School? You girls have raisins in your heads! You'd better learn how to milk cows and work in the fields properly because that's what you will be doing."

To Mia, too, this subject is like a red flag. "Can you believe that they really think they will be going to a university? Always keeping their noses buried in books and acting smart, they are! Don't you girls know that we lost a war? You will never see the inside of a university, you won't even get near the outside of one. Who do you think will let you in—the Russians or even the Americans if they ever come? And who do you think will foot the bill? Your days of being high and mighty and spoiled are over, and you might as well get used to the idea right now."

Marianne and I finish the breakfast dishes in silence, exchanging glances instead of words, and get out of the kitchen before another eruption. But as always the verbal slap has hurt.

"Just because they are older they think they know everything, especially that dumb broad from next door. But Mia should have better sense. You don't believe there is any truth in what they say, do you?" I ask Marianne.

"Forget it! Mia may just be jealous that she has missed the boat and is stuck here as the wife of a small farmer. If that isn't what she wanted, she should not have married a farmer. I am convinced that everybody has a right to choose his way of life and to be happy in his own fashion. To me her kind of life wouldn't be worth living."

"But when the chance to choose is taken away, as it is from us now, what then?"

"Oh, you of little faith! *Tempora mutantur.* What doesn't change is what is in us and how determined we are to make something of it. I sometimes think that we are born with certain hopes and aspirations, and I intend to make mine come true, no matter under what circumstances."

I feel closer to Marianne than I have in months because I need her positive outlook into the future to enliven my brittle spirit of defiance.

Between the comings and goings, the talk, and the chores in house and garden, a food-conscious eye is always turned toward the general store across the road by the bridge and toward the butcher shop next door at the tip of the delta where the road divides. Staples unreplenished in weeks past have dwindled, and at the storekeepers' discretion old stock is sold on a first-come, first-served basis. A loaf of bread and any meat at all are a treat because Mia doles out her supplies sparingly.

Most of the time, meals are a monotonous repetition of mashed potatoes, salad greens from the garden, and milk. When Mia makes an egg flan, no matter how large, it is never large enough for everybody to be satisfied. When bread is available, it is spread with a sticky dark syrup, like molasses, made from boiled sweet turnips. Sometimes Russians take over Mia's kitchen, frying slabs of meat and mountains of potatoes, and the left-overs provide a feast for everyone after the cooks and eaters are once again at a safe distance.

Occasionally stray wanderers still stop by, begging for something to eat and a place to rest on the road to nowhere. One of those was of special interest to me. Looking down the road one day, I spot the familiar blue *RAD* dress and red head scarf on a girl walking toward me. I know her! She had been with me at camp in Czechoslovakia and as one of few exceptions among the Silesian girls had been assigned to hospital service in Prague. How I had envied her "good fortune" then!

"Marga, what has happened to you?" I call out to the obviously exhausted, solitary figure.

Startled, then glad to see a familiar face, she follows me inside and asks to stay for the night. Listening to her, I realized that the adventures of her group of *RAD-Maiden* have been far more hazardous by comparison than mine.

"The soldiers got ready to leave and took us with them on their trucks. We made it through Czechoslovakia, way over to the western side," she tells. When the Czechs seized their vehicles and their belongings, they continued on foot. Strafed by low-flying planes, they took to the woods by day and tried to make easier progress by night.

"It was like trying to find our way out of a mouse hole. We came so close at times, but we didn't make it across the border. That's when we decided to split up. I have been walking off and on for almost two weeks, trying to get home."

Now, within a few kilometers from her home, she is in near panic about the fate of her family. Her father, a teacher and *Ortsgruppenleiter* ("local party leader") is bound to have been arrested.

"I hope they have gotten away. But how, then, will I ever find them?"

Detained by heavy rain until noon the next day, she

strikes out again full of fear and hope. I feel sorrier for her than for myself because she may really be all alone.

May Devotion

As far back as I can remember, the month of May has been a chain of lovely, sentimental church services. Some or all of the family would walk through the spring evening after dinner to a church or chapel for half an hour, rarely longer, of litanies to the Virgin Mary and hymns sent forth like love songs through the open windows. Fresh flowers in abundance, fragrant and bright, and the wax of lighted candles would scent the church, mingling with the incense at the final blessing of the Most Holy Sacrament. The little children would sit on the steps of the side altar dedicated to the Virgin, and the tunes they heard became as familiar as folk songs and nursery rhymes, indelibly inscribed in their musical and religious memory. They would be tucked away from one year to the next, much like the memories and rituals of Christmas and the happiness they stood for, to resurface again in May to joyful recognition.

May in the land around Glatz without May devotions is unthinkable. Even the collapse of a nation and the rule of an atheistic power are impotent against tradition. On evenings, when the Russian menace presents no immediate threat, people flock to church from throughout the village that stretches for several kilometers along the highways. From the inn at the crossroads, church is only a few steps away—a curve in the road, across the bridge, and up the well-trodden stairs to the gate. How comforting to retreat to a sanctuary where peace and silence reign until the organ breaks in with rousing chords! With or without faith, the congregation draws strength from each other. They revel almost sensually in the hymns about love and purity and supernatural beauty and find release in jubilant song. When the priest intones the litanies, the members of the congregation join more fervently than ever before in the plea *Bitte für uns* after every invocation.

For the second evening in a row, we hear the Voice, the smooth, strong resonance of a young male voice breaking through the high tones of the females and the hoarse base of a few old men. How long it seems since we heard a young German man speak, let alone sing! Aunt Gretl, who is a frustrated songstress, is as fascinated as we girls to whom the sound signals a potential distraction in our commune, all-female save for the Russians from whom we must hide or disguise ourselves. And having found him in church would surely allay the most conservative questions about his character. Aunt Gretl finds the man who belongs to the Voice, and as easily as with any stranger in the gregarious good times of her past, she draws him into conversation and into her circle of new friends.

Father Nightingale, as we dub him for his song and the small beaked nose in his pleasant, narrow face, is a refugee priest from Upper Silesia who, after weeks of wandering through Czechoslovakia with a small group of his parishioners, has interrupted the trek home until the situation there becomes more stabilized. While his people are scattered on farms, he lives at the rectory with the stodgy old village priest and his housekeeper.

Preferring more lively company, he comes to visit us and, being young himself, he particularly likes to associate with us girls, always ready for a laugh to offset the prevailing tense mood.

Perhaps because I am looking for a substitute for my brothers; perhaps, except for rare instances of the old closeness, because Marianne's and my sister's alliance shuts me out at times, I am in need of someone to talk to: I am drawn to him from the start, and he seems to enjoy talking to me particularly. Forgetting that he is a priest, or maybe because he is a priest, I can open my thoughts to him uninhibitedly. He seems so wise and intelligent, so experienced and compassionate, ready to dispel a doubt with a hearty laugh and just as willing to delve into philosophical depth and search for new insights.

Without telling him how it started, I admit to him my estrangement from the Church and God. Raised under Heia's tutelage in a fervently Catholic house, as I grew up, I was exposed to other views of God in my studies in school and, of course, to Nazi philosophy. But I remained clinging to the formalities of our faith, even loving the splendor of rituals and religious art, and was envious of anyone who mistook form for substance. I could no longer accept the articles of faith unquestioningly but merely as a symbol for the existence of some divine force. The Commandments, far from being a divine decree, meant to me a moral guideline necessary to keep order in the community of human beings. The question of good and evil, of right and wrong, troubled me throughout my precarious relationship to Mother, whom I refused to accept as a substitute for Mama. I could not pretend feelings for her that I did not have, and resented being reproached for my attitude. In the war years, the killing and persecution and claims of "just cause" on all sides of the conflict fueled my confusion further. Gerhard, who had once been a faithful little altar boy, broke with the Church in his teens. I admired his honesty and, like him, groped for answers.

Without confiding any personal particulars, I sense Nightingale's understanding.

"We tend to confuse doubt with guilt because by others we may be judged guilty. But there is an inner right, our individual standard which applies only to each of us, that remains beyond the reach or judgment of others."

He can't know that, as he talks to me, he is setting me free from an enduring pressure.

"If you can't trust in God, trust the strength in yourself." I am reminded of the "divine spark" in each of us that Goethe had seen in all living beings. Perhaps, I am not as distant from God as I had felt myself to be.

He hears much of what I don't say to him and seems to

recognize the hidden grief for our dead that I don't express, making me in Aunt Gretl's eyes an unfeeling monster.

"Not everybody reacts alike. If this is your way, keep a laughing face over a crying heart—I do know you like to laugh."

Annemie and Marianne tease me afterwards, when Nightingale and I have quietly talked, and accuse us of being in love. I laugh with them and at them with the purest conscience in the world, without telling them what a comfort he is to me.

The rectory where he lives is only a few steps away from the inn, almost within whistling distance. On this Sunday afternoon Nightingale whistles at close range underneath the open window behind the chestnut tree. A raincoat slung jauntily over his shoulder, he is keeping a date for an afternoon walk. We invite him up, just as the first drops of rain dampen the prospect for the planned outing. As on other occasions, we settle down for one of our long conversations that might take any turn. The others lose interest as at other times when the discussion becomes too serious or abstract.

He and I are steeped in such concentration that we fail to hear the heavy tread on the stairs. Marianne and Annemie have scurried into hiding in the other room by the time I hear the steps on the landing. A lone Russian stands in the door as I am poised for flight.

A calm order from Nightingale: "Sit down!"

I sink back on the chair, heart pounding. Authoritatively, possessively, he places his hand over mine on the table. The soldier saunters in past the row of beds, eyeing us curiously. Nightingale motions him to a chair, never taking his eyes off him. Is anything said? In what language? I am only aware of the calming pressure of his hand that conveys such confidence and affection that I am no longer afraid.

How long does the Russian sit by us? The men shake hands and he is gone. Nightingale exhales audibly, smiling at me:

"You see, everything is all right."

Even after the shower passes, there is no thought of walking in the woods today because the presence of one Russian means that more are about. Long into the night I puzzle over the scene of the afternoon, wondering what becalmed the soldier's taste for mischief—the Roman collar? the hand that claimed me? Nightingale's supreme serenity? In a flight into childhood faith, I visualize Nightingale sprouting the wings of a guardian angel and hovering over me.

When we walk with him on another occasion, Mother and Aunt Gretl come along to enjoy his company. In the thick woods above the village, on paths carpeted with fir needles, we freely breathe in the fragrant mountain air, and nothing is real but the moment. Far away from anyone's hearing, we break into song, Aunt Gretl's alto intertwining with Nightingale's lead and our voices fluttering lightly along. After years of marching songs with a combatant flavor we revert, as if by prior agreement, to immortal folk and wander tunes. We return refreshed in body and mind.

A few more visits from our unusual friend, then a Sunday on which he delivers a sermon at high mass that seems as honest and warm as an intimate conversation, devoid of pomposity and artificial piety. To say good-bye, he walks us home from church, falling behind while talking to me so that I, too, have to slow down.

"In these uncertain times people meet and lose each other again. I want to know what happens to you." With that he gives me his address which, to me, seems an empty but touching gesture.

"By the time you get there, if you get there, maybe the mail will work again," I skeptically give him my promise to write.

None of us likes to see him leave. From our upstairs window we watch and wave to him, as he turns once more on the bridge. Then the slender black figure disappears behind the rectory gate, taking with him the glow of his serene humanity and the joy of his song—flown like the bird whose name he shared that May.

To Lose a War

Unwanted Guests

Day by day we live in fear once again. Day after day nothing happens. When we return from hoeing root crops in the outlying fields, one of the women goes ahead to reconnoiter before the girls are allowed into the village. There are whole days when we huddle upstairs, escaping reality by reading voraciously, one ear listening for the dreaded sound of steps. When the downstairs rooms are full of soldiers, the women move among these with deceptive composure, wait on the Russians, and watchfully try to avert their attention from the dark stairway.

Fear is always present. It flares into panic at tales of atrocities—mutilated nude bodies tossed by the wayside—a woman nailed spread-eagled to a cart and gang-raped while bleeding to death from her wounds—horrible diseases spread to their victims by sex-drunken Mongolians. The tales die of their own unfathomable violence, but once heard, their memory festers on and leaves a residue of fear ever after.

Mia, who speaks Czech, somehow manages to communicate with the Russians, and this communication seems to elevate most encounters to a more civilized level. She has discovered that her little blond cherub-daughter never fails to delight the soldiers. While keeping her close, she permits the child to be talked to and cuddled by the strange men. Whether a national trait, as some claim, or simply the longing of lonely men for their families, no Russian we meet or hear about hurts this or any other child. The mother's linguistic efforts and the daughter's innocent charm seem to deflect some of the potential danger from the household.

One morning a lone Russian officer with his orderly sits in the public room talking to Mia and playing with the child on his lap. Personnel carriers pull into the yard, and soldiers pour into the house. Before they even spot the officer, he stops them with a command. From the brief, harsh exchange, Mia gathers that the officer has claimed the house for his quarters and sent them packing. Off they roar down the road.

Mia showers the man with effusive thanks before he and his orderly, shortly thereafter, also drive away.

Often in the evenings, we sit around the large kitchen table in the company of neighbors and an elderly couple from Berlin who are among our regular visitors. He, a scientist, majestically bearded, with pince-nez and walking stick, holds forth with flowery analyses on the past and alternately lapses into hypochondriacal recitations on the present effects of his reduced living standard on his heart condition. His wife flutters about him with constant concern, interrupts soothingly when he gets carried away by his own oratory, and interjects sobering down-to-earth observations. Of their three soldier sons, one has been killed, one is officially reported missing, and the third somewhere in the nowhere-land between war and peace. Enjoying the company of young people, both have grown fond of us girls. Marianne is their favorite.

"If my wife weren't by my side," teases the man, "I would tell you that I am in love with you."

"Wouldn't it have been wonderful if one of our boys had met her and she could have become one of our family," comments his wife, underlining the man's affection while diverting it to a more restrained context. Pleased, Aunt Gretl nevertheless demurs:

"What good will it do any of our girls now to be pretty and educated! Just look at them—in their field-hands' camouflage they are scarecrows of their former selves. What a pity!"

"Nothing can detract from the charm of a pretty girl," he insists. "Watch out that someone doesn't carry her off to the altar before you know it. Sooner or later, some of our young men will come back. Keep her in disguise so that the wrong kind won't find her out."

The flattery is not lost on Marianne who beams from one to the other speaker and is sure to examine her appearance with renewed confidence later before the mirror upstairs. All of us girls bask in the kindly, refined presence of the Berliners and revert to being well-bred young ladies when they are with us. Often after they leave, we replay their conversations and mannerisms with affectionate mimicry, creating an endless situation comedy around the devoted couple. Aunt Gretl with her flair for the dramatic joins in the fun and laughter, and even Mother, embarrassed by our benign disrespect, chuckles to herself.

The dying sound of motors breaks into one of these relaxed evenings—it's time to disappear upstairs. We can hear coming and going of heavy footsteps and loud voices, and later the clatter of pots and pans in the kitchen. There are times when the presence of many people in apparent harmony seems to make the intruders feel comfortable and peaceful. These soldiers, having brought in food supplies, signify that they mean to prepare their evening meal here, and everybody present is invited. They seem such a friendly and harmless lot that one of the women calls us back downstairs to eat with them. We drift in one by one, as if by accident, and start setting the table to keep busy and feel less conspicuous and more relaxed. The meal is lavish by our standards, and the Russians evidently enjoy the satisfaction of their guests and their own magnaminity. Attempts at communication in sign or any other language lead to bursts of hilarity, as we sit in the mixed round.

After dinner the Russian cook opens cupboard after cupboard until he finds glasses. He puts a jug of vodka on the table. Tonight we are friends and everybody must drink! Over and over he fills my glass. Cautiously sipping the burning liquid, I try to spill most of it unnoticed. The adults sense that the friendliness has gone far enough. We are told to clear the table, start washing dishes, and somehow get lost. The old scientist, whose bearded dignity intrigues the Russian soldiers, draws the cook into a sign language discourse, all but hypnotizing him. While one of the women continues clattering with pots and pans, we slip from the kitchen into the flagstoned hall and upstairs into hiding.

The cook points to the place where I had sat, starts shouting for his *panienka*, and storms out the door to look for me—fortunately the wrong one; there are four of them leading from the kitchen. He staggers back angrily. The adults gang up on him, urging him to drink with them, and somehow calm him down. After that, even the most congenial Russians get to see us only by accident.

As the weeks pass, traffic starts flowing in an easterly direction. Occasional truck loads of German POWs alternate with Russian convoys and long columns of infantry whose chants sound wild and truculent. Sometimes the inn is like an island in a sea of Russians. These withdrawing troops are bent on booty and souvenirs, and many a farm is picked clean as if by locusts or, as the Russians are nicknamed, *Maikäfern*. The troops remaining behind will form the permanent occupation force or, as it turns out, will be in temporary administrative control.

For times when escape from the house is impossible for us girls, we have devised a hideout in the room next to the *Lazarett*. Two huge wardrobes all but fill the narrower wall at one end of the room. We have laboriously shifted them forward by a foot and placed a cabinet at right angles against them, leaving a narrow slit between it and the wardrobes. At a danger signal we squeeze through the slit and against the wall behind the wardrobes. Short of a sneeze to give us away or someone lying on the floor to see our feet, we cannot be detected.

Once again Mother rushes upstairs with the now familiar cry:

"Quick, quick! Russians looking for quarters!"

We four potential victims of rape—Marianne's little sister included—squeeze between the cabinet and the wardrobes and slide into the space behind the wardrobes. Outwardly calm, Mother has barely settled into a chair when the door to the vestibule is opened. Russians look into the *Lazarett*, then into the cramped room where we are hidden. There is some discussion during which we dare not breathe, then the soldiers apparently opt for the room with many beds. After several trips up and down, they seem to have settled in. We remain standing like statues pressed between the wardrobes and the wall.

Much later, when the other women come upstairs and

the natural sounds of several people cushion our movements, we come out of hiding. That night, no one undresses. Somehow each finds a place to curl up in a soft chair or on a pad on the floor, and we doze fitfully wall to wall with a room full of Russians, who occupy our beds. Some of the voices next door sound feminine. It is strangely comforting that these Russians have brought women of their own along.

Next morning, when the military vehicles are about to leave, we cautiously venture downstairs and cannot resist taking a look at our nightly neighbors. The thought that the Russians might have chosen the other or both rooms sends chills down our spines while we rejoice at our deliverance.

Once again nothing has happened, but there is always a next time—tomorrow? next week? in an hour? Danger, real or potential, surrounds us like the air we breathe. Our very lives from day to day are structured by the high and low tides of fear.

Father and Mama

Heia and Franz

Sunday afternoon outing

With Franz and Gerhard

Annemie

Marianne

Religious procession

Gerhard

RAD *Maiden*

'lag raising at RAD *camp*

Franz

5

Peace Without Honor

Changing of the Guard

For days the military convoys have been roaring through the village. Hardly anyone ventures out, and the fields go untended. When there is a break between columns, an oppressive silence reigns, more paralyzing than the noise of the traffic. Once we rush to the window because we think we can hear a German marching band. The rhythmic sounds come closer and closer, and the glint of metal instruments darts in the distance. When the musicians come into sight, they are Russians, of course, yet the music they play has the same triumphant and rousing quality as the marches through which the tread of German soldiers rang for six years.

Sometimes odd hand-clapping and music drift into our upstairs prison so strange that it draws us irresistibly to a window overlooking the yard. There are soldiers strumming triangular string instruments, shouting and singing, while others, sometimes only one, leap and swirl and squat in wild and captivating dance. The exuberance of the strange men is in such contrast to our joyless existence that we momentarily experience vicarious joy. There seems no doubt that the rumors of Russian withdrawal are true. The troops are heading east, for home—no wonder that they dance and sing!

On a rather quiet day, Mother suggests that it might be time to look after the apartment in town for repossession if the troops have vacated it. I volunteer gladly for reasons of my own—to steal a few hours of solitude, visit Heia, search for friends. It is now possible to go part way by train, reducing the time of exposure on the open road.

The family mission is unsuccessful; the red flag still flutters from the building, and a soldier stands guard at the gate. The town seems restless. Too many people are about but no familiar faces among them. During the past week there has been a steady influx of Poles who claim to be rightful citizens of this land by the Potsdam decree of the Allied Powers. The Polish red and white flag flies from the city hall.

Against my aversion to approach the Poles in their official capacity, and thereby acknowledging it, I go there and find that many of the offices are staffed with Germans. I listen to them with disgust when they address each other with *Genosse*, which has a distinctly communist ring to me. Even in Hitler's days, *Herr* Meyer was only turned into *Parteigenosse* Meyer in the context of party affairs and not in civilian offices. I hate being among the *Genossen*, staying only long enough to get a work release from the city office based on my certificate obtained by Mia, and an entitlement to ration cards in the village. Thus accepted by the bureaucracy, I am a legitimate citizen of the village at last. Of what country, I don't know!

Heia receives me with a mixture of pleasure and alarm:

"I am so glad to see you unharmed. But be careful! The Poles are no better than the Russians. I don't know what all this means, but things are likely to get worse, with both of them persecuting us!"

Ignoring Heia's apprehensions, I pursue my other errand: I must find out what has happened to my best friend, Erika.

"You have reappeared! From where?" she rejoices, and

we account for our experiences since we last met at Landeshut. The camp unit to which she had been assigned was released even later than mine, but she was lucky enough to catch the last train home.

"What do you make of all this commotion that the Poles are causing here?" I ask her.

"Pay no attention! They are just flexing their muscles. The Russians will keep them in check—why should they want to share their victory with the little brothers whom they heartily dislike anyhow?"

"Sometimes I wish we had stayed in town," I remark wistfully. "At least here you can watch what is going on. In the country we live behind the moon—nothing but gossip and speculation and grubby work."

"I don't know that it makes any difference where anyone is now. Here or there, it is such a useless existence, such a waste of time."

"Her restlessness is driving me crazy," complains her mother to me.

"A person has to do something besides staying out of harm's way. We ought to be in Vienna right now in our first semester, as we had planned, remember? Instead we are idling our lives away getting nowhere, maybe never getting anywhere."

"Children, it has only been a few weeks. Your life is still ahead of you," her mother counsels, probably not for the first time, unsuccessfully.

"What life? Do you really think we still have a future?" I voice the questions that are on everyone's mind.

"Germany has recovered from other bad times. It may be longer after this terrible disaster, but we must be patient. Where are your courage and pride?"

I want to listen to Erika's mother as an antidote against Mia's woeful predictions and Aunt Gretl's dwelling on our losses.

"Your mother may be right," I speak up with revitalized spirit. "This can't last forever. It can't get us down unless we let it, and no matter who lords it over us, I am still proud to be German."

"Like *Deutschland, Deutschland, über alles?*" mocks Erika, and then more seriously: "Can you imagine a Germany without soldiers and fanfares? I can still see them marching through our streets, and the snappy little lieutenants we used to flirt with, how sharp they looked. Even now and never will I listen to a bad word about our soldiers. They fought against unbelievable odds to the very end. Thanks to them, no Russian set foot in our town in combat. Whoever may be at fault that we lost the war, it wasn't theirs!"

In Erika I have found a kindred spirit as always. To my question: "Will we become Polish if the Poles really should be given Silesia?" comes her resounding reply:

"I will never opt for them! Never!" Quite the answer I wanted to hear.

"Getting out of the house will do you some good," urges Erika's mother, "but not for long and not very far."

We stroll off together as in old times. Erika nudges me: "Do you see what I see?"

There is no mistake, the Russian woman coming toward us is wearing my suit. Mother had sewn it for me, combining plaid cloth with left-over solid material from one of Father's suits.

"It doesn't look at all bad on her—maybe a little tight," I answer lightly and really don't care. Face to face with a thief, who is unaware of discovery, is no more than a little disconcerting when there is neither chance for recourse nor desire. Possessions have little meaning any more when survival is at stake.

We part in the middle of town. On my way to the train station I enter the church that stands massive and defiant in the street life surging around it. Like an island of peace, the cool, faintly fragrant edifice receives me, shutting out the noise and brightness of day—a place of rest and solitude. People are kneeling in some of the pews, and unexpectedly for this time of day the bell rings in the beginning of a service, and the organ comes to life. The mighty instrument weaves a festive, harmonious melody which I have never heard; it sounds like a hymn but no one is singing. Has sorrow silenced voices even here where they used to be raised to the glory of God? When the organ sweeps into a repetition of the hymn, a lone male voice joins in, then more and more. I hear words, in a language I cannot understand, penetrating my consciousness like swords and shattering my prayerful repose. Angry tears well up in my eyes, and I have to fight the urge to run from the house of worship and the presence of these people who surely desecrate it with their piety. Are these not the same people who have come here for vengeance, who, contrary to the most fundamental principle of Christian love, violate the person and property of their neighbor? How distant God must be, how detached from his creation to tolerate such worship offered to him, and to listen to prayers asking his blessing on violence committed in the name of justice! I feel betrayed and deprived of a refuge that I still cherish with childlike naïveté, confused once again by a world that lives by double standards and expedient interpretations of absolute laws.

"Not even you are safe from them," I complain to God. "Now you, too, have forsaken us."

Realizing my irrational claim on a personal God in competition with friends and foes, my anger melts into sadness at having lost intangible values I cannot even name. The hymns float about me, the music touching my tortured soul, and with a strange new detachment I must acknowledge their beauty.

After mass I walk slowly, as if saying farewell, down the length of the aisle between ornate columns that seem to reach into eternity, past gilded side altars dedicated to saints whose lives and names once seemed like an extension of my family, suddenly a stranger in the familiar house of a strange God.

I wish Erika were still with me to help me regain my balance. The sense of being alone and a stranger pursues me, and for once I can't wait to be among my people in the refugee household in the village.

Father and Son

The village has a Polish mayor. Someone has complained to him that too many people are assigned to Mia's farm for work, and he has come to her for an accounting. As the end result, Annemie is sent to the manor house, now occupied by a Polish administrator, to work as a live-in housemaid under the direction of the German manager's wife, and Marianne must work on another farm while continuing to live at the inn.

"See what trouble I have gotten into, trying to do the right thing by you," cries Mia. "It's getting too much for me: A person isn't even master of his own house any more." Shaken up by the unwanted official attention, she secludes herself for days and bursts out crying when anyone wants to talk to her.

Aunt Gretl, too, is in one of her black moods.

"We are not even welcome in my father's house." Her complaint is directed less against Mia than the general turn of events. "We lost our beautiful home in Breslau, and now this trouble!"

I feel like stopping her with a sarcastic remark—sure, you had a nice home, but it wasn't all that beautiful—but she is off on one of her usual plaints in superlatives:

"My father was the richest man in this village," which I sincerely doubt, "and under his very roof we are going to starve yet if we don't get thrown out first. I wish I hadn't gotten rid of that gun—I can't take much more."

Marianne, in her mother's vein, joins in:

"And I, his grandchild, am no better off than a beggar! I can't stand being poor! Do you really think there will be an inflation like the one after the last war and our money will be so much trash? When you adults talk like that, as you did last night, I want to die because without money there is no hope of ever improving our lot."

Once again I am hopelessly out of tune with them. What we have or don't have means little to me; nothing can buy back life for our dead or the love we must do without, and nothing can restore the joy of life which lies buried or in shambles.

"I am so hungry for music, for just one concert, and I want to dance, dance, to forget this misery for just one night."

"How can you even say that?" gasps Marianne. "How heartless can you be!" Aunt Gretl makes a speechless gesture of insanity in my direction.

It is time to withdraw before the pack tears me apart, to hide my irrational yearning for a past when joy was possible and could still bring relief from despair. If only I could get away from these people with whom I seem to share little beyond the physical proximity under one roof! We used to be at ease with each other, even enjoy each other's company. Sometimes I can't even understand Marianne any more, as obviously she can't understand me at times. Living close together under severe conditions accentuates the differences between us, and we clash constantly without meaning to.

And yet, we are better off than many others who still roam through the country in search of a refuge. Weary wanderers are such a common sight that no one spares them more than a fleeting glance. Mia's old relative who tends the children especially dislikes seeing one of them approach the inn. Although she is not an unkind woman, they present a threat to her when they ask for something to eat.

"We don't have enough for ourselves," she whines but rarely sends them on without a drink of milk or a slice of bread if they beg desperately enough.

When two dusty, sunburned men, neither quite civilian nor quite uniformed, cross the bridge and enter the inn, she is again about to start her plaintive chant. Mother breaks in with a shout:

"My God, is it really you? Eugen! Egon!" and hurries toward the older one with the thinning hair over his tanned brow, his trousers gathered loosely over a remembered paunch. He opens his arms wide with mock exuberance as if to embrace her and the familiar house and all he finds assembled in it. The other, the boy, hangs back, smiling with embarrassment and hopeful anticipation of welcome.

The news of their arrival flies through the house. Two of our men have come back from the fringes of the last desperate defense of a lost war. Most remarkable, neither has changed beyond recognition in physical appearance and personality. Two men are joining this world of women and enemies! They are proof that miracles still happen.

The man, too old for the draft, was conscripted to serve in the *Volkssturm* in defense of his Upper Silesian hometown and was swept along with the retreating armies; the boy, too young for the draft, had been part of the youth brigade and had strayed among fleeing civilians and soldiers deep into Czechoslovakia and been stranded there. By sheer chance they met and escaped the rounding up of military prisoners, and together they had started on their faltering march toward home, or wherever.

Eugen the merchant—his slender hands are still soft and uncalloused under the tan of weeks on the road. When I look at the vagrant, I remember vacationing at his house where he presided at a table set with china and silver on spotless linen; I remember the delicate white of the guest room and the three boys who took turns escorting me to the sights in town. Now he has found the youngest, roaming on foreign roads, and knows nothing of the other two or their mother, his "beloved girl," who ruled the household with grace and warmth.

My own family's decline has been too close to me to observe with full awareness, and each progressive step has been blurred by the needs and tensions of the moment. Facing this man who has sunk from complacent wealth into abject poverty is like looking into a mirror that reflects how low all of us have fallen. The Russian steamroller has leveled to mere subsistence everyone in its path.

Reeling from the blow of meeting him like this, I am puzzled by his still indomitable spirit and air of confidence—a born survivor. I have learned that happiness does not last, but he claims that misfortune, too, is temporary.

"Nothing is final until we are dead," he proclaims. "Just look at yourselves, my pretty cousins, in your present disguise as farm folk! Look at the vagabonds my son and I have become! Isn't this an experience of which our soft life would have deprived us? The time has come for all of us to be workers of the fist," he announces, flexing his muscles, and his humor is so contagious that the bleak reality is transformed into a tragic comedy.

Mia, ever practical, wants to know what their plans are.

"Dearest, if only you will let us rest our weary bones in one of your soft featherbeds, we ask no more."

"That's all I can promise you as long as the house is mine. As soon as you have had a good night's sleep, you must find work—I am already in trouble with the authorities for harboring lazibones," says Mia ruefully.

"God bless your kind heart and all you hold dear," shouts Eugen in grandiose eloquence but visibly relieved.

Within days, father and son submit to work assignments "of the fist." Eugen, who never wielded anything heavier than a pen, becomes a woodcutter, and the boy, who was yanked away from his textbooks to bear arms he could not and would not fire, loads lorries in the local quarry. Eugen marches into the woods with an axe over his shoulder every morning and returns at the end of the day exhausted but never too tired to describe his labors and expound upon his new experience without bitterness or complaint. On his daily climb to the ridge he has designated spots where he stops to catch his breath.

Sometimes Aunt Gretl watches him pensively as he makes slow progress toward the woods, stooping low on the steepening rise.

"Come here," she calls us girls. "What does this remind you of?" Between hilarity and sadness, the path with Eugen's rest stops is given a new name—The Stations of the Cross of Saint Eugenius.

Touched by the retreating figure, a wave of loneliness washes over me with sympathy and self-pity. Is not each of us a lonely wanderer under a cross? Off and on since Father and Franz have gone, I have been plagued by a growing sense of abandonment and the realization that my life lies in my own hands—vulnerable and worth so little, a still-to-be-traveled wasteland covered by the rubble of broken dreams. While life has come to a standstill for us, time races on. Somewhere people are planning, working, learning, have goals and love and choices. I must break out of this stagnation, away from the prison of this time and place, into some useful activity.

Now and then we hear of someone who has struck out toward the west in the defiant spirit of do-or-die, in search of a future. I envy such a person's courage. But viewed in another way, is theirs not a selfish flight from adversity? What if all of us were to leave? Must we not stay to claim this land as ours? I keep recalling Nightingale's counsel to trust in God or in myself and never be tempted into rash action.

I hide my yearnings and indecision from the others and come to accept loneliness as an integral, inescapable part of my being. Like Eugen on his way to the woods, I must bear my cross and bide my time and, like him, I must walk alone.

I contrive to be sent on another reconnaissance in town and find Erika as much in need of me as I am of her.

"You girls aren't helping each other at all when both of you are depressed," says her mother. "It is time to do something to get your minds off your misery."

"Well, then, tell us what!"

And, indeed, she does. "Do you remember the private business school across town? I hear that it may be opened. Of course, that may not appeal to you—"

No, it doesn't, but it would be better than nothing.

"Why not?" Erika looks at me expectantly.

I hesitate, imagining the reaction "at home," but an intriguing thought gains the upper hand.

"Hey, then I would have to come to town regularly and could be with you," I grin at her.

Enrolling for courses in typing and shorthand, we feel, is the first positive step either of us has taken. We feel elated for having made a voluntary decision about our personal lives. Back in the village, nobody pays much attention to my foolishness for the time being. Mother offers hopefully:

"Then you can keep an eye on our apartment every time you go to class."

Heia's joy of seeing me every few days is of short duration. A month after my first venture into town, her welcome is nothing short of panic, and with reason:

"You shouldn't have come today. Haven't you heard?"

On the previous day, a Polish proclamation has been issued which orders the German population out by noon the next day, today. Only a few meek souls tremble with fear, others ignore the order as a cruel joke that has been staged in other communities where the evacuation order was rescinded as suddenly as it was given. But here it is still in effect. The provisional German city government and the Russian commandant have urged the citizens to remain calm. This morning the Poles have attempted—early and illegal even by their own ordinance—to clear a few residential blocks. Yet even billy clubs and rifle fire have failed to intimidate those affected, and Russian patrols have intervened to stop the Polish terror. A wave of fury and hatred is the only lasting result of the abortive evacuation attempt.

As much as I fight against acknowledging these developments, I fear that they indicate an irreversible change and that all Germans here live on borrowed time.

Still unaware of the tidings I bring, Aunt Gretl greets me in a cheerful mood:

"I hear a Nightingale singing!" and hands me a letter written in an unfamiliar hand and unstamped. Dated three weeks earlier, it tells of Nightingale's return to his home rectory, looted and abandoned. Not even passing through a countryside strewn with animal cadavers and human corpses could destroy his appreciation of the ridiculous.

Traveling on an open flatcar has its advantages: Lots of light, air, and sunshine. At night I slept on it covered with nothing but the moonlight—a mite cold—and on awakening was frisked by a Russian in a top hat.

A snapshot of him in happier days and a little paper icon revive in me the memory of him and of our talks. The printed legend on the icon reads: "Come, hold my hand. Be good, my child, and let the peace of God reside in you."

Sunday Visit

From Glatz, railroads fan out in all directions, linking almost every village and all of the smaller towns in the area to the city and from there to the fast long-distance trains beyond the mountain country. Since the end of the war, traffic has resumed only on a few mainlines, none of which passes through our village. But by the middle of June, service starts on a limited schedule on our route, too.

The local trains are short and slow, snorting and puffing out of a station, skirting the fringes of villages and traversing fields and bogs for short distances at a time, before the shrieking brakes signal the approaching next stop. Long before the train comes into view of another station, the bell on the engine peals a warning at every crossing of a field path, and these are so frequent that it rarely stops ringing. Ours is the second stop on a line that dead-ends in a health resort snuggling in the mountains.

We are used to hearing the resonant church bells in the village; they never failed to ring at the traditional times during the week and for Sunday services. The quicker, harsher clanging of the train bell startles the village out of its isolation. We are only too glad to speculate that conditions may be returning to normal.

On its first Sunday run in June the train brings Heia to us for a family celebration. It is Mother's birthday, but the irony of fate conspires to pair the significance of special dates in our lives: It is also the silver anniversary of Father's and Mama's wedding. Heia congratulates Mother politely but without warmth and loses no time reminding Annemie and me of the, to her, more important reason for her visit.

"Your parents were such a proud looking couple when they married twenty-five years ago. Just look at them," she says, pointing to their picture that I have set up on the dresser for the occasion. Father, shown in his World War I uniform, looks the way I like to remember him. Although I have only seen him in civilian clothes, he always carried himself as though he belonged in a uniform, and his looks didn't change until the last war overburdened him with work and worry. Mama in the picture is almost a stranger, because in my recollection she is a withdrawn, gray-haired woman who seemed to need more care than she could give.

"She was not beautiful but as fine and proud as a noble-woman when she was young," Heia reminisces.

To me Mama had always looked unremarkable and some-what old-fashioned. Seen through Heia's undying adoration of her, whom she had known since youth and had served for more than a decade, this flattering picture of Mama pleases me. I realize how often I have missed her, and to keep the hurt from showing, I turn to Annemie.

"You look as snobbish as she does in this picture, only prettier," I tease my sister who has inherited Mama's family's slightly hooked nose and fine bone structure.

"*Setz' dich über alles weg,*" Annemie strikes an arrogant pose, "then the world will be at your feet. You ought to learn that, *Lütte,*" she counters without malice, calling me little one to remind me how much more adult she always appears than I in spite of her younger age. Unaffected by her house-maid status at the manor house, she seems more the type to be in charge there and has already charmed her employers by knowing just the right mixture of subordination and submis-sion. She is quick and resourceful in everything she does, and rarely out of sorts. I admire her more than I love her because our personalities are poles apart. I have no doubt that she will always hold her own.

"And you look more like your father all the time," says Heia to me.

"And always were his favorite," adds Annemie, a touch reproachful as always when the score is not in her favor.

"Privilege of a first-born daughter," I grin at her.

"Girls, girls," laughs Heia. "Your parents would be pleased with both of you," ignoring for the moment what has become of us.

As always in Heia's presence, I experience a return to the secure world of childhood, as if the old woman held a magic wand that could still open every door and smooth every path. Now more than ever, Heia is indispensable to me, as indispensable as the memories of past happiness.

"They would be proud of you even now," she adds as an afterthought. "Sometimes I think they are better off not knowing what has become of their family. You saw how hard Gerhard's death was on your father. Losing him and then losing her favorite, Franz, too, would have killed your mother."

We are back in the present, caught again in the sorrows of the more recent past.

"The grave is blooming all over," Heia tells us sadly and means the profusion of flowers that her care has coaxed from the mound of earth. She tends Franz's grave like a shrine. To me, her simple statement exemplifies again the paradox that has mocked every shining day of this cruel spring because it says that beauty and horror, life and death are brothers that exist side by side without relation to each other. In turn, I succumb to the charms of one and the power of the other, but when they assail me in unison, the impact of the contradiction is almost beyond bearing.

"We don't want to waste this beautiful day indoors. It's so quiet and peaceful—come along," invites Mother.

We walk through the fields in the afternoon sun. The ripening wheat waves gently in the breeze, and the village lies far behind us in languid Sunday silence. We pick corn flowers, bright and blue, and red poppies from the edge of the fields, gather purple clover and white anemones, and all kinds of weeds designed with delicate perfection. These minute delights of creation are treasures no one can destroy or take from us because they always reemerge. Nature's bounty is the only lasting gift that everyone can enjoy and no one possess.

We walk Annemie to the manor house, and when the church bells ring the Angelus, the rest of us take Heia to the station just as the clanging bell chimes in to announce that the train is approaching down the meandering tracks. The scene, the sounds are deceptively like those of other Sundays when the family would spend a leisurely afternoon over coffee and cake with Mother's father, the old innkeeper, and hear the same bells, and meet the same train. But the resemblance is only a surface sham, and nothing is, and can ever be, the same.

I stay behind where I don't belong, and the train carries Heia away with her aura of childhood safety and the bouquet of wildflowers that are a greeting from life everlasting to one who passed into everlasting life.

The Apartment

I had suspected all along that my courses at the business school rankled Aunt Gretl and that sooner or later she would erupt.

"You have mounted the wrong horse, my girl. Who but a deluded teenager would think of going to school in times like these? Running away from work is what you are doing," she rants.

"The wrong horse is better than none. I'll ride it until a better one comes along," I shoot back. "As for shirking work, let Mia be the judge. She is the boss, not you."

Mia is on my side: "As long as you are here when we need you, I have no quarrel. When harvest comes—" she starts the sentence and I finish it for her:

"Then I will skip classes, I promise."

"Gretl, she is doing nothing wrong," intercedes Mother.

136

"Can't you see how important the lessons are to her? And she can keep us posted on developments in town."

I am relieved to have won this round and can continue going to classes and, much more important, seeing Heia and Erika in the process.

The Polish ordinances in town change rapidly. The first one that called for the evacuation of the entire German population is <u>amended</u> to exclude Germans who are granted a residence permit by the Polish city commandant personally—those courting his favor. Next modification: Those voluntarily renouncing their German citizenship and swearing allegiance to Poland are allowed to stay. Then, the evacuation order is to affect only those who have taken up residence in town since 1939. Finally, only unemployed Germans and those in nonessential jobs will be forced, at the discretion of the Poles, to leave. The only fact in the mounting confusion is a steady increase in arrests and beatings and the confiscation of property at Polish whim. With the rural work permit in my pocket, I feel relatively unthreatened at this time.

The street to Erika's house is barred; armed, square-capped militiamen stand guard. A woman pulling a haphazardly loaded handcart is allowed through the barricade, and I recognize in her the owner of the apartment house.

"I don't know where they have gone, but they won't be back," she replies to my inquiry about Erika's family. "I packed as much and as long as this lot let me," she snarls. "I am the last one to leave."

If it weren't for meeting Erika at the business school later, I would have lost track of her. Soldiers are everywhere—Poles, Russians, sometimes at cross-purposes and exhibiting barely contained hostility toward each other. For safety's sake in the company of Heia, I check on the situation in my old neighborhood. The reconnaissance seems more promising than at all the other times. A relaxed Russian guard, who has seen me repeatedly, somehow communicates that the building would be cleared by the troops at five. Mother comes to town on the afternoon train. We go to our house but the same guard is still posted and voices a regretful *Nyet*. With a desperately articulate sign language we convince the Russian that we will scrub and sweep. Amused as much as worn out by our persistence, he lets us pass.

We have been warned by others who have witnessed signs of Russian occupancy to expect bedlam and to abandon our hopeless mission altogether. Thus we expect the worst, but our idea of the worst has not prepared us sufficiently for reality. Shocked to the point of collapse, we survey a battlefield—heaps of refuse through which broken pieces of furniture rise like cliffs; stench gags us, almost driving us to retreat. Ragged remnants of clothes, crushed dishes, books, pictures torn from frames—rubble in every room. We can't look into the dining room because it is locked. Above all, the nauseating stench that emanates from the largest and totally wrecked living room! Spoiled contents oozes from splintered canning jars, garbage of indefinable origin is mixed with unmistakable human excrement, and dried stain of urine discolors crumpled paper and rags. We wade into the dump with care and poke at some of our all but unrecognizable belongings. Overcoming our revulsion, we penetrate to the lower layers and discover unharmed books, loose photographs, bundles of old letters, odd pieces of silverware, an occasional unbroken dish.

Perhaps a systematic foray into the disgusting wreckage will unearth a few mementoes of value only to us that no one will deny us. We gather into backpacks and baskets any and all things not soiled beyond bearing. The wardrobes with doors torn from their hinges are empty, their contents looted or mixed in the stinking heaps. A piece of silver braid protrudes from under one of them; I wrench it free, recognizing the shoulder piece from Franz's dress uniform, and slip it into my pocket to be preserved forever with a few old letters and the Iron Cross as his pathetic legacy.

The guard barely glances at us as we pass, and after unloading our pitiful treasures with Heia, we invade the chaos once more.

On the train ride back to the village I tell Mother how

the guard had indicated five o'clock as the time at which the Russians would leave.

"He may have meant five days from now instead of five o'clock," she guesses.

"But he pointed to his watch. I am sure he meant five o'clock."

"Do you think that he was showing you at what time he would go off duty? He was making a date with you!" she cries out in horror.

"And then you came along and spoiled the fun, thank goodness. I hope we'll never find out what he had in mind," I shudder at the possibilities.

Next morning we start out early in hopes of finding some useful things after all. Our basement compartment held crates of household goods stored there against the danger of air raids. With broken china under scattered coal and rotting potatoes crunching underfoot, we spot a turned-over trunk, empty but sturdy and useful for transporting more at one time than we could otherwise carry.

I take a tour through the building. In a distant wing of large offices, I discover our chaise longue and one of our beds in obvious recent use. It seems that the fury abated in the stark, functional rooms; only the apartments must have incited the victors to vengeful vandalism. Behind gaping doors I see neighbors digging dejectedly through their own refuse.

Mother is close to tears when I return. "Don't ever walk off like this on your own. Just because nothing has happened to you so far does not mean that it can't or won't." She still sees in every Russian a rapist or a murderer, as far as any of us girls are concerned, but seems to consider herself immune.

"I wish you wouldn't worry so much. I saw only very few soldiers and stayed out of their way," I try to reassure her.

While we comb through the destroyed rooms of our apartment, a bemedaled man with a proprietory air unlocks the door to the dining room—probably its occupant and a man of some civilized standards, because it looks almost intact. Encouraged by the unexpected find, we make him understand that we have designs on "his" realm and, with his shrugging approval, pack the trunk with some linens and dishes. We even remove a few chairs, but an unfamiliar guard at the gate raises objections until persuaded by our benefactor to let us pass. When we return for another load, the dining room with its coveted treasures is locked again and remains locked. We spend exhausting hours half-heartedly sorting through the remains of the other rooms until the menacing presence of an unfriendly soldier drives us away.

Two days among the ruins of our worldly possessions have sapped our strength more than the physical effort alone could have done. What have we gained? Was there any point in amassing even these few personal things for the new life which is bound to come eventually, in burdening ourselves again with things so easily destroyed and so hard to lose? Despondent and tired though I am, I record in my diary how cruelly our home had been defiled, as if I could ever, ever forget the scenes of senseless destruction and the odor of putrefaction.

Harvest

The zenith of the year is already past, and piercing sun at noon and long, light, balmy evenings have followed the restless, sparkling days of spring. The grain in the fields sways heavy with its ripeness, yearning for the reaper. The villagers heed the call of nature as in every other year: This is the time to crown their endeavors of months past, and even the crops that had lacked proper care at times have brought forth ample yield.

A young man who turned up in the village from who knows where has been sent to the inn to help with the harvest. In another life he was sports and recreation director for a large industrial firm, and now he brings the spirit of his former job to us. He has a positive, sunny temperament, likes to joke, and often sings while he works. Grumbling and bad-mouthing stop when he is around, and even Mia's surly old servant brightens in his company.

From the first hushed morning hours, we work in the fields. While he guides the team, we gather into thick sheaves the grain that the horse-drawn mowing machine has felled, tie them with a few strands of the still fresh and flexible straw, and lean the secured bundles against each other in tepee shapes to dry for a few days in the blistering sun. The sharp stubble left standing in the soil scratches our legs and arms as we bend in the motion of gathering, sweat stinging the tiny wounds. Hours of doubling over and straightening up turn our backs into aching agony on the first day, making every movement on the next morning a painful contest between the desire to refuse and a conscious demand to obey. But each successive day increases the resilience of every muscle, and our bodies become machines tuned to the rhythm of the big blades that cut the grain in broad swaths ahead of us. The sun and the hot breeze envelop us and paint the exposed skin an angry red that subsides at last to a glowing tan, deeper and more natural than the cream-covered broil of lazy summer days of other years.

Long, straight lines of huts made of grain rise from the stubble field, and we view the hard work of our hands with justifiable pride and satisfaction. After the heat and toil of the day we are at peace at night.

"Harvest isn't as bad as everybody tried to paint it for us," I confess to Marianne, who has spent a similar day at her assignment on another farm.

"Nothing is as bad when everybody is busy and we have our minds on other things instead of tearing each other apart. Sometimes I am disgusted with myself and the others for the thoughtless things we say, aren't you?"

"Sure I am," I agree with her. "Even though I mean them at the time—sometimes not even that because I say them out of spite—I wouldn't have dreamed of shooting my mouth off like that in normal polite society."

"That's just it: Nothing is normal, and the masks are down. We will all have a lot to forget."

Nights of deep sleep—the healthy sleep of physical exertion—are untroubled by the dark images of past and future, and the days are so full of sweat and common purpose that nothing matters but the task at hand.

Sunday is a day of rest even now, and no one begrudges us girls the small pleasure of a few lazy hours. With blankets and books we settle by the river where bushes and high grass hide us from the road. Children's voices drift through the Sunday silence, and through a break in our green abode we watch the sunlight dancing on the water as it leaps over rocks and fallen trees, and see small children splashing in the quick, shallow current on the other side. Sometimes a heavy step crunches on the gravel of a nearby path, but even this seems devoid of threat as we lie prone and perfectly still. Between us and the brilliant summer sky rises the richly leafed crown of a mighty tree behind whose trunk the span of the bridge gleams under the sun and white-washed milestones stand in blinding, glaring light. The bushes to the side of us border on a fairy-tale garden where flowers grow in wild, exuberant abundance. Our quiet world of green tinged with the bright touches of summer lulls us into dreamy languor. On the wings of dreams come memories—

"You wore the dress you have on today when we had the fiasco at the *Eis-Café* in Glatz, remember? When you sat down, with a corner of the drape caught on your chair, and the rod came crashing down on the glass table top—" I start to giggle.

"And it took most of my vacation money to pay for the damages!" recalls Marianne. "And then we went home and composed a silly poem about the incident to send to our 'victory candidate' Hannes."

Hannes is dead, says our silence.

"You haven't been so dark-tanned," Marianne comments, "since that summer in Breslau when people stopped us on the way from the beach to ask where you were from because you were too dark to look like a German."

"What a lovely way to get a tan, swimming and playing tennis," I reminisce. "That was the summer vacation Alfons spent his leave at your house, and I fell for the blue-eyed, curly-topped sailor."

"I had to let you have him because he was my cousin," concedes Marianne.

"Oh, the power of love," I am making fun of myself, "I wouldn't admit being scared and swam with him across the Oder River. You and Annemie had more sense and watched from the beach."

"No less scared than you, believe me."

Our sailor, my first love, went down on the *Bismarck*.

"Do you remember our last all-day excursion across the *Heuscheuer*? Just the two of us, and we didn't have to be afraid alone in the woods. We started out from Wünschelburg and took so many breaks on the climb that we missed the afternoon train on the other side of the mountains. By the time we got home at midnight, Mother and Father were on the brink of calling rescue squads and police and God knows what!" I recall.

Marianne laughs: "Maybe that's why it was our last all-day excursion alone!"

"You remember Rudi, don't you, my dancing partner? He is from Wünschelburg. One time Erika and I during vacation wanted to surprise him and her boy friend, who was also from the area. We surprised them all right—with two girls evacuated from Berlin, lolling at the swimming pool."

What has happened to them? Are they even alive? Every memory of fun times in the past turns into a sad memorial or apprehension.

"Can you imagine being in this pretty spot here without listening for every sound on the path, with the feeling that the world is in order and waiting for us?" Marianne's feelings run as rampant as mine in the chasm of what is and what could be and what has been.

When we donned our dresses from another life to celebrate this day of well-earned rest, we asked for an illusion of well-being and leisure. But the things of the past become incongruous in the present, preposterous. Pensive hours are treacherous and breed disturbing thoughts more than they cure. The bittersweet flavor of a lazy Sunday afternoon lingers on until another harvest day buries nostalgia under its strenuous demands. And for weeks exhausting days alternate with leaden sleep at night.

Harvest's End

Es schienen so golden die Sterne.
Am Fenster ich einsam stand
und hörte aus weiter Ferne
ein Posthorn im stillen Land.
Das Herz mir im Leibe entbrennte.
Da hab' ich mir heimlich gedacht:
Ach, wer da mitreisen könnte
in der prächtigen Sommernacht!
        Joseph Freiherr von Eichendorf, *Sehnsucht*

These nights the moon drops a silver net over the darkness. We like to sit by the open window of the *Lazarett* and let our favorite poets speak to us. With sonnets and love songs we pay homage to the timeless moon and immerse ourselves in the romantic dreams of men long dead, dreamers whose words now evoke indefinable longing.

Füllest wieder Busch und Tal
still mit Nebelglanz,
lösest endlich auch einmal
meine Seele ganz.
. . . .
Ich besass es doch einmal,
was so köstlich ist.
Dass man doch zu seiner Qual
nimmer es vergisst.
        Johann Wolfgang von Goethe, *An den Mond*

Under the spell of the whitened night and the enchantment of the verses, we are carried into a realm of undiluted feeling and are lifted out of the limitations of our unhappy existence. Very still and strangely disturbed, we build a bridge of waking dreams that crosses over into a world of sleep.

Moments later, reality intrudes with jarring noise. Fists hammering on the door downstairs, men shouting; then one of the women telling us to get dressed in a hurry. The victors have come to claim the completed harvest.

Within minutes, Aunt Gretl, Marianne, and I are walking through the moonlit village to one of the large farms that has been designated as a threshing station. The Russian commando pursues its mission with fervor. The threshing machine is fed the golden grain day and night and continues to spew the plump kernels into huge bags. A human chain transports the bundles from ceiling-high stacks to the monstrous machine on the barn floor. Trucks are waiting, ready to carry the harvest from the village to silos in a distant land.

Overworked from the ceaseless demands, the threshing mechanism grinds to a halt with almost predictable regularity, and suddenly there are too many people milling about where moments before their hands were too few. Between feverish activity and idleness the hours pass. In the dead of night, the crew of soldiers and civilians feasts in the farm kitchen on the heartiest meal we have enjoyed in months. No doubt the village livestock has been reduced by a few more animals to supply the succulent roasts before us.

Not long after starting up again, the threshing machine cranks and rattles in protest and stops again. Every pause fills Aunt Gretl with anxiety because she fears that idleness might breed mischief.

"You girls have to vanish," decides Aunt Gretl when the repair work appears to be unsuccessful.

"How do you think we can get away from here? If they catch us, we will be in worse trouble than if we hang around," I object.

"Follow me over there when no one is watching," she motions with her eyes toward the bales of straw stacked behind the barn. "You get up there and stay there until I signal you, understood?"

145

We grapple with the bundles of straw until we manage to climb to the top layer out of sight from below.

"Your mother never runs out of ideas," I admit with grudging admiration.

"I wish you two wouldn't fight all the time. She doesn't mean half of what she says." Marianne is burrowing a hole into the warm straw. "Your accommodations for the night are ready, *gnädiges Fräulein.*"

"I am glad we are in this together," I say to her, meaning more than just this moment. The bonds of friendship will prove stronger than this time of dissension, I feel sure.

Above us the star-holed cover of the night sky, we fall asleep in our fragrant hollow. When the fog banks roll up from the nearby river, chill moisture settles over us, awakening us to the gray morning sky. Aunt Gretl is still standing guard near the base of our bed of straw. No one has missed us, and we join unobtrusively into the gradually resuming activity. The sun stands high and bright when we go home. Someone remembers that today is Aunt Gretl's birthday.

When we leave again in the evening, we have more to worry about then the threshing shift ahead of us. Egon has not returned from work in the quarry. If he were hurt as once before, someone would have surely notified us; it turns out that he failed to report to work that morning. Since young men are favorite targets for Russian chicanery, our worry is not without reason. A boy in the neighborhood, who had recently returned from an American POW camp, was beaten savagely; we don't know why, probably neither does he.

A day later Egon comes back, dirty but unhurt.

"Where in the world have you been?"

"I spent a day and a night locked up in somebody's potato cellar," he grins sheepishly.

"Whatever for?"

"Well, yesterday on my way to work this Russian bully stopped me and wanted me to go with him. I showed him my papers and tried to make clear to him that I was on my way to work. By the time some German explained to me that the

Russian was snatching people off the street for his threshing operation, I had gotten kicked around and the Russian had me by the collar. And off he dragged me to that cellar. Am I ever hungry!"

Threshing is not as bad as a thrashing, we conclude. As members of the night crew we have to work on several successive evenings; even time is turned topsy-turvy in our haphazard lives.

At that, we thank our fate for the twelve-hour threshing shift in the cool of the night. Many other girls have been rounded up to herd cattle from surrounding villages to points east. When at last these return after days of long marches, they tell of hot and dusty roads among the cows that went unmilked for days at a time and collapsed from pain and heat, and of nights spent in fields with their restless charges and even less desirable companions.

The cattle drives and grain transports deplete the wealth of the village. Summer's toil has been for naught, and the certain need of winter fills us with dread. For days we walk over the bare stubble fields to pick the few forgotten stalks, gleaning a pitiful harvest for ourselves.

Happy Cargo

Indian summer, gentle and a little sad. Hazy mornings, dipped in dew, linger long and cool. When the sun drinks up the dampness, the air becomes transparent and light, retaining a brisk freshness even during the hottest part of the day. A deep blue sky stretches over the fields of yellow stubble, over emptying gardens and tree tops where tired leaves are taking on the hues of fall. Dusk settles early, blanching the sky and drawing mist up from the meadows by the river.

On a day like this, the pulse of the village beats faster because we are participating in an unlooked-for drama of happiness. All day trucks from the east roll by. When the first ones came into view loaded with German POWs, only a few villagers were outside to wave to them. But the joy of seeing them, as they were coming from the east and proceeding west is passed on by word of mouth until the sides of the roads are dotted with women and children waiting for more to come. And they come at intervals all day long. Each roaring in the distance stirs us with expectant excitement, and a great cheer and shower of blossoms flutter over the weary, smiling men in passage.

Sometimes a vehicle halts by the gasoline pump at the inn. Then we rush back into the house for water and fruit to refresh the men on their way home to distant provinces in the west.

Though defeated and dishonored, these men are still our soldiers, and showing our enthusiasm for them is a gratifying protest demonstration amid the oppression of the so-called liberators who have "liberated" the village from its wealth and all hope for the future. As always when German POWs have been herded through, usually on foot and in the opposite direction, I search for a familiar face among their ranks. Someone I have known will surely come back. But even the faces of strangers, these fortunate ones on their way to freedom, stir joy in me and a heart-felt thanksgiving for their deliverance.

Three thousand of them, it is said, pass through the village on that day, three thousand individual lives saved from the dire fate they might have shared with thousands of others. For one day, we celebrate the homecoming of strangers as they rush past or briefly pause. For one day the village is lifted out of its doomsday mood.

This unexpected link to the west gives me a unique opportunity. I scribble a note to Father's old friend in Bavaria, telling him of our plight and asking him to serve as our letter drop if, more likely when, we should become separated in an attempt to escape from Silesia. When the next truck slows at the inn, one of the soldiers accepts it from me. I feel that I have taken a first, if unsure step into an opening future.

Polish Rule

The Polish infiltration of the village is slow to start but picks up momentum with every passing week. A lone Polish woman appears at Mia's door to claim the inn for herself. Outraged, Mia deluges her with such a torrent of Czech and German that the whole household is alerted by the commotion and descends like a dark cloud on the intruder. The woman retreats with a threatening remark on her lips and is never seen again. On other farms, Polish masters have already crowded the owners into back rooms or off the property altogether, depending on personal animosity or compassion.

Every trip to town becomes a test of nerves. Bands of militia roam the streets. They are young and brazen men, propelled into the role of victors overnight and without merit of their own, who thoroughly enjoy the taste of power. Since all Germans are required to wear white arm bands, they are marked prey for these willful adolescents and can be easily identified and herded off for any type of labor or humiliation. The few German men in town, most of them well beyond their prime or found physically unfit for military service during the war, bear the brunt of degradation and terrorism. Sooner or later, each is arrested on whatever pretext comes to a Polish mind, and even those released after hours or weeks of interrogation or hard labor come home broken men.

Anger and contempt for Polish measures make me determined to ignore the danger in town. I begin once more to pay attention to my clothes and go about my business with a show of confidence that, deep down, I do not feel. A sweater or coat folded over my arm and the expediently slipped-down white arm band obscures my identity; when this trick fails, I rely on my rural work permit for salvation. Except for minor incidents, the ruse proves successful. But I cannot shut out the impressions of what goes on around me.

Guarded by armed militia, a column of civilians marches by, men of my hometown, in Polish custody. Suddenly the sad troop is in disarray; I see an emaciated, white-haired marcher slump against his neighbors, who catch him in the fall and drag him across the sidewalk. Propping him against the wall of the nearest house, they attempt to lift the ashen face that bears the marks of torture. Before the militiamen can drive the staring pedestrians to the opposite sidewalk, I recognize in the two helpers a teacher and the kindly pharmacist who, at personal risk, had welcomed into his home some of the disowned nuns from my former school. Their suits flap loosely about them, and the only color in their haggard faces is the shadow of sprouting beard. Cold, impotent fury clenches my fists to see good men mistreated for no reason other than the accident of their nationality.

The local prisoners are incarcerated in the dank basements of old houses, without sanitation and even minimal comfort. For a slice of bread and a bowl of broth they are meant to endure labor and torture—if they survive. Heia is so disturbed by these conditions that she does something about them, little as that may be. She tells me how she walks close to the barred basement windows and drops small bags of food through them from under her gathered apron.

"Heia, they will nab you, too," I warn her, frightened for her but at the same time admiring her courage.

"Oh, don't worry about me, nobody is paying attention to an old woman like me. If I can help a little, it's my Christian duty to do so."

No one would suspect a person like her of breaking the law or think the frail, gray woman capable of heroism.

Her employer's business has been appropriated by the Poles, and so have the best rooms above the hardware store. When her mistress sees me, she dissolves into tears. Seeing the good woman's despair after the scenes I just witnessed, shatters my composure. What happens to others, to see them suffer, always seems to have a much greater impact on me than my own misery. Heia, with overflowing eyes, must strike another blow.

"You have seen for yourself what is going on. Nobody is safe, and everybody has to look out for his own skin. I want you to understand what I must tell you," she takes my hand

and continues: "Your father was well-known in this town, and that in itself is hazardous—"

The man of the house is afraid that any link to someone who might be in disfavor now, like Father, presents a danger, and he does not want me to come to his house.

"He is a good man, you know that. He is thinking of his family. You mustn't let this upset you. We must meet and we will, even if only for a few minutes at the train station or to go to the cemetery together. After a while he will calm down; it's just now, with all these arrests—"

Heia keeps soothing me but all I can hear is another door swinging shut—my world is shrinking and slipping away.

Eventually and inevitably, a Polish family moves into Mia's house. They arrive, four of them, with a few personal and household goods. Eugen and Egon must vacate their room and move into the tiny chamber under the sloping roof that used to serve as quarters for the Ukrainian field hand. The Poles seem to be as ill at ease as we on whom they have been foisted. Mia elicits their story: On their sweep through Poland, the Germans overran the family's home in the Beskide Mountains and resettled them in the Ukraine; now the Russians have displaced them from there, and in the new "Polish" territory they are to receive reparation for their losses. How many on all sides of the conflict have become inanimate balls in the hands of uncaring political jugglers? Is everybody a victim?

After a few days of subdued living under the same roof, sharing meals in the kitchen at separate tables, and working—if not together, at least in the same enterprise—a visit from one of the most ruthless and unpopular Polish administrators disrupts the tentative truce. He objects that Mia's family and relatives are still sleeping in white featherbeds; the Poles should have them! In the kitchen he disdainfully stirs the cauliflower soup and demands meat for his people. At that, Mia's patience and composure snap, and the stout, little woman blasts the man in every language at her command. He leaves, far from intimidated, but the message he leaves behind is clear without the aid of words: If the seeds of dissatisfaction he tried to sow are not tended by the Polish family, their superiors will bring them to fruition with pressure and force.

By the end of August, the area is solidly in Polish hands. Despite the indisputable evidence, the official proclamation of the Inter-Allied Commission, confirming Polish annexation of the region east of the Oder-Neisse line, strikes the German population as a devastating surprise. The time of rumors and hope is over, the die has been cast.

The most immediate question is that of livelihood. Stores now demand Polish currency for their wares, the train fare must be paid at the rate of one zloty per kilometer. From where is the money to come? The noose is tightening, and some cannot wait for slow perdition.

Even though I must walk to town to save the price of a train ticket, I attend classes whenever I can. Erika's father, who had acted calm, almost aloof, during the few times I visited at their old home, has attempted suicide and became hysterical when quick action saved him.

"That is the last straw," she confides. "My mother doesn't know whether to pity or despise him but she can't take much more."

I walk with her from school to her cramped refugee quarters nearby, and she urges me to come up.

"It's easier when other people are around. I can't stand seeing my father in disgrace and as listless as he is now, and my mother at the end of her tether. They will pull themselves together in front of you."

Erika's mother has been waiting for her.

"Come in, girls, sit down. It's just as well that you are here," to me, "to hear what I have to say. I have decided that as soon as your father is fit to travel, Erika, we are going to leave. In a few days he should be well enough. If we stay, I am afraid he will try to do away with himself again."

"So that's it," concludes Erika without betraying what she thinks.

"The worry here and worrying about your sister from whom we haven't heard since she left was too much for your father. I pray that she is safe in the Russian zone but we need to find out."

"You could have gone with her while you could still get out instead of sending her by herself to your relatives in Saxony," says Erika.

"Child, we couldn't go without you. There you were in the *RAD* close to the front—we had to wait for you. How would you have found us? At the time it seemed the right decision. Who could have known that the area where we sent her would be overrun by the Russians long before we were."

"I wonder what it's like over there," I muse.

"No Poles, and it is Germany still, even though the Russians occupy it," Erika expresses the thoughts in my mind as well as hers.

"How will you get there?" I ask her mother, ever eager to gather information about getting out.

"I hope mainly by train if we raise enough money on the black market. With luck, claiming relatives to go to should help us get an entry permit. I don't think the Poles will stop us since they are threatening to throw us out anyway."

I leave them, bereft as though my friend had died and more than ever torn between staying and following their example.

Within the next few weeks, the rooms at the inn are beginning to be subjected to a game of musical chairs that will be played over a period of months. The Poles want more space for themselves and for visitors, too, and every expansion symbolizes an increase in authority. A family to whom Mia had sublet a large housekeeping room is evicted; their furniture, of course, must remain. In anticipation of a similar fate, we pack our belongings and wait. A time-bomb has started ticking—if only we knew the hour for which it is set.

Back from the Dead

Returning from town one afternoon, I am stopped by an acquaintance near the entrance to the village:

"Hurry home! There is good news waiting for you."

"Convince me," I challenge the woman.

"I just heard that Mr. B. is back from the war."

Miracles still happen. What if the grapevine had twisted the news and the man were not Mia's husband but Father? My conviction that Father is dead cannot withstand the surge of wild hope and longing that propels me toward the inn in breathless expectation. But this greatest miracle of all is not in store for me.

In the public room of the inn I see a lonely figure in something vaguely resembling a Russian uniform. He sits at the table by the tile stove where the regulars used to have their friendly card games and mugs of beer. He sits without moving, and I am struck motionless by the sight. Now and then, the breeze from the open window touches him and makes him shiver as if from an icy wind. The only other sign of life is a steady rivulet out of the corner of one eye, tracing a shiny line along the parchment nose and joining the saliva that drools from the slack, half-open mouth. The hairless skull hangs low on his chest, arms dangle between his wide-spread legs, and a drop from his chin falls at regular intervals between them on the floor. Except for the drip and the chill that trembles through him occasionally, he resembles a broken statue, with rags tossed over its ragged edges. The visible parts of his body—the gaunt head, the lifeless hands—are carved in the design of a skeleton too recently dead for decay to have shed the skin that stretches tightly over every protuberance. Sunken eyes glisten feverishly in their hollows, glazed, vacant, dead. Like a scarecrow bleached by sun, wind, and rain, the figure is of an indefinable color, skin and rags blending to an ashen gray.

The greeting has frozen on my lips. What is there to say to a man who seems no longer human? whose instincts, surely, more than any conscious decision have carried the remains of his body to the place where he used to be a man? who lights like a homing pigeon on the very spot that was his point of departure into regions beyond nightmare? No flash of recognition or acknowledgment of another presence emerges from the once gregarious innkeeper who liked to roar away from his gasoline pump on a heavy motorcycle. In an irrational reversal of my earlier thoughts, I tiptoe by him, no longer wishing the man to be Father, and shaken and ashamed of my revulsion by the sight.

In the kitchen, the others are huddled in a helpless hush, not knowing how to approach this intruder from the netherworld who has given them no sign of being aware of where he is or who they are. Mia, who in weeks past has managed the invasion of refugees and who has stood her ground against Russians and Poles, is almost out of her mind and without a clue about how to cope with the repulsive creature who is her husband. By his sightless, immobile posture he has rebuffed every attempt to move him. We are frightened because he may be mad, even dangerous if he has any strength left, or too sick in mind and body ever to return to being human.

His obvious state of near-starvation at last gets Mia's practical mind working. She carries a bowl of steaming soup to him. When she comes back, she whispers, horror-stricken:

"He can't even eat any more. You should have seen him sinking his whole face into the soup and slurping it, not even using a spoon. And he kept trying to drink it while it was coming back up. It's terrible!"

Food is the only thing he has acknowledged so far—food he can no longer tolerate.

"We must get him to bed," counsels Mother. She and Aunt Gretl and Mia somehow carry him to the bedroom behind the kitchen, strip the reeking rags from his body, and bathe and swaddle him like an infant. After that we don't see him for weeks, except for Mia, but his presence hangs like a pall over the house. Mia, growing pale and wan in her care, stays with him constantly, watching over his deathlike sleep and feeding him pap at regular intervals. He lets everything happen to him in a trance without a will of his own, too weak to resist or to demand anything, incapable of speech, but she proves strong and determined enough to make him live and coax him to respond to her.

The man who emerges from the room where he is reborn is a mere shadow of the hulking, robust innkeeper, but he is almost fit to reenter the community of human beings, sit at table with us, and react at least with his eyes to the activities around him. He finds his speech, haltingly and sparingly at first. But the stories he could have told about his perilous journey remain buried forever, sunk in the River Lethe on which he drifted until his wife pulled him ashore. And no question ever ruffles the waters over their deep, merciful grave.

Fool's Paradise

Although nothing remains of Erika, the lessons at the business school are a legacy to which I cling tenaciously as the only part of life that is truly of mine and my friend's making. During the harvest I had stubbornly kept up with assignments without attending classes; now I can go to town again regularly, but always on foot—the train ride has become a luxury beyond my means. I don't feel in greater peril on the open road than I do in town or in the village, and I relish the sense of freedom on my solitary walks.

On the straight stretch of road outside the village, where fields extend in both directions and the only house in sight is an old, abandoned toll-house, a droshkylike vehicle overtakes me. A Russian soldier holds the reins, and next to him sits a girl whom I vaguely recognize as someone from the village. A little way ahead of me, the droshky stops. As I try to pass it, the droshky moves across my path to the opposite side of the road. I return to the right side of the road, but again my way is blocked. I don't like this game. Every time I change sides, so does the droshky. By now we have progressed, weaving across the road like drunks, to the driveway into the toll-house. The Russian motions me in that direction. Fighting panic, I ask the girl:

"What's going on?"

The Russian looks me up and down, making me wish for invisibility. The girl, who gives the impression of knowing him well, starts talking to him, ignoring me. How can this

Dorfpflanze ("country bumpkin") communicate with him, I can't help wondering. Suddenly the Russian's expression changes to an arrogant smirk. What now? He says something to the girl, who turns to me, copying his expression:

"He says he can have any girl he wants, and he prefers me to you. You'd better run while you can!"

He cracks the whip over my head, making me jump in spite of myself, and the droshky disappears down a field path in a cloud of dust before I can command my shaking legs to resume walking. I am as far from the village as I am from town. If I turn back, I will have to explain why I am back so soon. If I do that, I will never be allowed to go to town by myself again. I keep walking in the direction of town. Nothing has happened to me, and no one will ever hear of this incident from me!

By the time I reach the business school, I am already apprehensive of the way back. Take it easy—one thing at a time is enough, I force myself to concentrate on the squiggles on my note pad. The group of students has gotten smaller; there are many reasons for absence these days, all valid excuses—if these were required; circumstances are beyond control. Class proceeds as though we lived in orderly times.

We lift our heads from the notebooks, disturbed by noises closeby—loud voices, calls for help, wailing, steps approaching and rifle butts banging against the door. Militiamen with guns drawn invade the classroom, herding between them the large family of the teacher. He turns pale at the sight of his daughters, seven of them, and his wife at the mercy of the soldiers. Without ceremony or explanation, the typewriters and other business machines are carried from the room by some of the soldiers, while others hold the people in the room at gunpoint. They silence the lamentations of the teacher and the crying of the girls with threatening gestures, demanding to see each person's identification. The local girls are told to stay where they are, only I, with my work permit from the village, am sent away because they have no jurisdiction over me.

Rain pounds the pavement, drenching me, as I run toward the center of town, frightened by the second close escape in one day and enraged at yet another willful abuse of power. The Russians have intervened to help in similar incidents, and foolish hope carries me to the Red headquarters; they do not want to understand me, refuse to hear me out. At the Polish militia headquarters I get as far as the guard, who cuts into my story with righteous indignation, saying that the soldiers have every right to search the premises of suspicious persons. I flee from the open hostility in his voice. I have one more card to play. Through the downpour I race to the house where I know the son of the powerful Pole for whom Annemie works to be billeted, one who has a reputation for greater compassion than most. The officer is out.

Back at the business school, a guard with a machine pistol drawn for action discourages any approach to the beleaguered building.

Later I stand before the officer whom I consider my last hope. Forcing my voice into a polite, calm tone, I request that he see to the safe conduct of the people held prisoner in the school. Since he has come into the hall to talk to me, other officers gather around and enter into the conversation. Whatever possessed me to come here? It's no use, and he, visibly embarrassed to be singled out by this strange girl for a mission of mercy, formulates in civilized German the most common of all subterfuges: Other pressing commitments prevent him from granting my request. I withdraw, apologizing for having troubled him. Inside I cringe with humiliation, imagining the men laughing behind my back. My wounded pride is only slightly assuaged by knowing that I had begged for the sake of others. I vow never again to ask for favors, never to acknowledge hurt at Polish injustice.

The end of my private enterprise—the business school is confiscated and does not reopen—leaves a void that clamors for a substitute of my lost personal pursuit. Once when delivering a letter from Mother to someone in the last remaining German army hospital, I happen to meet a former teacher who is now pressed into part-time service as a kitchen aide there. While she continues peeling potatoes, she tells me that three of her former students visit her regularly for literature study. She invites me to join them in her home.

"It won't do for all of you to arrive at the same time," she cautions me, "because meetings of any kind might be suspected of subversion. God forbid that we should be raided! So we have worked out a schedule to stagger the arrival, and you must leave separately as well."

The house in which the teacher lives is located on a busy thoroughfare and the entrance open to view from many windows across the street. The prospect of this newly discovered activity delights me, and I accept her invitation enthusiastically.

If we mean to meet for two hours, coming and going at intervals costs additional time, but we don't mind. For a few hours once a week we pretend to be students again, turning in assignments and discussing them in class. We discover that even previously known works have gained a new meaning for us, deepened by our own unrealized maturity. They have not changed—we have.

One of the plays we read is Schiller's *Don Carlos*, and one quotation from this drama shines brightly like a precious jewel ever after: "*Ein Augenblick gelebt im Paradiese ist nicht zu teuer mit dem Tod bezahlt.*" In a humble measure, the literature classes become for me moments in paradise, and in an equally humble measure, the chances I have to take on my lonely walks to town are the exacted payment.

Buried Treasure

Whether in deference to the still ailing innkeeper or from a kind of compassion born of their own experiences, the Polish family at the inn coexists with the other residents in relative harmony. The tall, rugged-looking man, stern and uncommunicative, takes on the customary male chores, tinkers with tools and machinery in the barn, and during the potato harvest breaks the soil so that we can pick the potatoes from the field. Gradually, the woman, whom everybody simply addresses as Pani, spends more and more time in the kitchen with Mia, who feels threatened in her domain. Very soon, when neighbors come for their jugs of milk, it is Pani instead of Mia who fills the jugs and receives payment. Mia is clearly being replaced as mistress of the house, and to retain squatter's rights on her own property, she steps aside resentfully but without useless and harmful resistance.

One morning a woman from the apartment house knocks on our door, visibly upset:

"Let me come in and sit down." Her hands shake so badly that the milk in her jug is sloshing over. "Just now in the kitchen downstairs I heard music when I came for milk. That's so unusual, with no one having had a radio in months, that it made me feel kind of happy. Do you know where the music was coming from?" She barely restrains herself from shouting: "From *my* radio on *their* window sill! I nearly fainted." She looks as though she still might.

Aunt Gretl jumps up from her chair: "You mean they found our hideout? Oh God, they must be taking the whole place apart looking for loot! They will take everything we have!"

What an eerie night it had been during our earliest time in the village when this woman, Aunt Gretl, and I had struggled to hide our combined possessions! As the bombardment of Breslau increased, months before the city was encircled by the Russians, Aunt Gretl had shipped trunks with linens, clothes, and household goods to her parental farm for safekeeping. Just being under lock and key wouldn't keep them safe from the Russians, she feared with good reason, and she wracked her mind for a foolproof alternative. Where was a place large enough and completely secret? Then it came to her that in the course of some past remodeling of the barn a double floor had inadvertently resulted in one corner of the hayloft. No one unfamiliar with the building's history could possibly suspect the hollow space between the old floor and the new. Since climbing a ladder to the top level of the barn, carrying heavy, bulky weights, would be impossible, Aunt Gretl took the woman whose attic wall adjoined the barn into her confidence. This woman was physically a very strong person who could be of much help; she was also anxious to share the hiding place with us. By loosening some boards in the attic wall, we made an exit into the hayloft. The two women convinced me of the safety of our secret cache so that I hurriedly packed a rucksack with my prettiest dresses from dancing lessons, some jewelry, and the earliest diaries to stash with their possessions, among them the neighbor's radio. How we had labored and sweated, and how smug we had felt after the job was done!

"How can they possibly have discovered that place?" puzzles Aunt Gretl. "Who has the time to poke through bales and bales of hay and then through every single crack between the boards?"

"I tell you who!" I cry out, incensed. "That nuisance of a kid who has nothing better to do than to bother us and think of mischief."

I detest the Poles' twelve-year-old son who tries to pinch us girls, who bothers even his sister, and acts brazen to everybody.

"I could wring the damn brat's neck," snarls the neighbor.

"Can't you just imagine their glee when they discovered our treasure trove," hisses Aunt Gretl. "The nerve to flaunt our things before our eyes!"

Not many days after this incident Aunt Gretl announces a scheme to keep some valuable papers out of their reach and a few essential clothes for her husband, who is missing at sea. As usual, in any undertaking that she believes requires strong nerves and hard work, she drafts me to help. Marianne is to be involved, too, although her mother claims that she gets tired or hysterical too easily to be of much use. The more hands we have the quicker the job will get done. Buoyed by the prospect of a minor victory over the Poles, we girls are game.

Before dawn we tiptoe downstairs in stockinged feet and out of the house. Each shoulders a burlap bag with things to be hidden, and in one of them is a short-handled spade. When we hurry up the path we have nicknamed The Stations of the Cross of Saint Eugenius we do not pause until the woods hide us from view. Perspiring freely despite the chill of the damp, leaden morning, Aunt Gretl leads the way to a point in the woods that she believes she will always be able to identify.

"Mother, let's be sure," says Marianne. From the familiar jog in the path, next to a stand of raspberry bushes, she counts the rows of trees, turns right and counts again.

"Between the tenth and eleventh tree in the eighteenth row. I am going to write it down as soon as we get home."

We take turns, hastily digging a hole in the soft forest soil, tightly fold a rubber sheet around the things to be buried, and sink the bundle into the deep hole. Burial goes faster than the digging. Aunt Gretl jumps when an owl calls nearby.

"Romanticism at its best," quips Marianne nervously.

We trample down each layer of loose dirt until it is firmly packed and very little unused soil remains. Over the grave we scatter dry needles of evergreens and broken twigs. From afar a dog yowls, sending chills along our spines. Could the Polish forester be about this early in the morning? Or had we taken more time than intended or estimated? We cannot risk being discovered at the scene of our "crime" and run along the ridge to where the woods are thicker and full of dry broken branches. We hurriedly stuff the now empty bags full of kindling wood to have a ready explanation in case we are discovered, with only the spade to give us away. As if on cue, it starts snowing. Whatever happens now, the woods will keep our secret.

The barking continues to sound as distant as before, but near the edge of the woods a voice halts us. Reckoning is at hand. The forester demands to know who we are and where we live and what we are doing in the woods. During her explanation Aunt Gretl opens her bag for him to see the proof of what she says. I hold tightly onto mine, silently praying that he won't look into it and discover the spade that I carry.

The man lectures us on what he considers trespassing on Polish state property and insists that we accompany him to his station so that the incident can be properly documented. We plead that we must get back to the farm for morning chores—that is why we had come to the woods so early. No matter, he is adamant. Fortunately, his German is sufficient for a conversation of sorts, and Aunt Gretl is a master at drawing people out. Marianne and I are frightened into silence.

The formalities at the forestry station amount to an entry in a ledger for three bags of kindling and a stern warning to obtain a permit in advance before ever gathering wood again.

At last we reach the inn, weak-kneed and trembling, with bags of kindling for which we have no room. If really expected to perform chores immediately, we would have had to plead illness.

Strange Bedfellows

A few bright late fall days bring a pleasant diversion in the person of Konstantin. From the time he arrives at the inn, Pani wears a smile on her face. Her daughter Tasha loses her reticence and laughs and hums, and whenever her eyes rest on Konstantin they are like a caress. He is the oldest son and obviously adored by the whole family.

Blond, blue-eyed, and wholesome looking, Konstantin appears in the hated militia uniform, and at first sight of him we instinctively recoil. To harbor militia among us seems the ultimate insult and an ill omen. For a few days we simply ignore him and evade any friendly overture on his part.

But Konstantin is on leave and means to enjoy it, and along with his uniform he sheds all threatening aspects. When two of his friends come to visit, one speaking German, the young men, through the interpreter, try to communicate with us girls and charm us; they get as far as learning our names. After that, whenever Konstantin meets me, he bows flirtatiously and enunciates my name. At a meal I reward his playful attention with one of the few Polish words I know when I serve him soup. This brief *prosze* sets him off on a burst of appreciative laughter and talk of which I only understand his friendly attitude.

He follows me by the hour, carries water to the stable with me, waits for the dishes to be done so that he can entice me to help him learn German from a Polish-German dictionary. He tells his mother and Mia that he will come back next time with documents to take me with him to England where he is a member of the Polish brigade. Mia translates.

"That's what he thinks," I remark to Marianne in English and laugh out loud for the first time in many, many days, shaking my head in consternation at such an unthinkable proposal. But Konstantin is unperturbed.

At meals, after the Polish family is served, we sit down at our separate table for our separate meal. Sometimes Konstantin brings his plate and squeezes between Marianne and me, indicating that his *duzy apetyt* needs to be appeased with our meager fare, and sometimes he loads a plate at the Polish table, insisting that we be his guests. Tasha watches the fun from her place, loving her big brother with her eyes. How well I can understand Tasha's devotion to him! And since he is never very far from me, neither is Tasha. Errands into the village become a threesome; although at first put off by his uninvited attentions, I accept them, a little flattered and resigned at the same time, as guarantee of safe conduct wherever I need to go.

But I refuse to go to the Polish movie theater in town alone with him, as he suggests; instead, we talk Konstantin into a family walk to the woods. Marianne flirts with him outrageously, diverting attention from me, until his head is spinning, literally and metaphorically, between two laughing girls. For a few days we are all young together and full of laughter, ignoring the bitter events that brought us together. Konstantin leaves, but Tasha has come out of her shell and remains friendly.

The bright interlude, so harmless and uncompromising, causes me acute pain on reflection. How easy it would be to be tempted into forsaking one's principles, into forgetting the desperate seriousness of the times! When next I stand at my brother's grave, I am overcome with remorse and shame.

The inn again subsides into a dreary routine, and the divisions between its occupants surface once more. In another round of musical chairs, we lose our *Lazarett* and are relegated to a small housekeeping room situated at the back of the house above the stable and looking out over the straw-covered manure pile in the farmyard. A definite advantage is the cooking stove there: It keeps the room warm and spares us the contact with the Polish family even at mealtime—perhaps, the latter result matters to the Poles as well. Mia's family is no longer in the house but in a tiny apartment next door, and Mia seems actually relieved that she no longer has to watch Pani in the role that is hers, Mia's, by rights. But, then, rights as we have known them are things of the past.

An old menace that we had all but dismissed from our minds creates new tension in the village. Russian troops arrive in great numbers. The meadows around the village are once again furrowed by the tracks of heavy vehicles. Looting and violence occur, with Poles and Germans equally victimized.

One evening Tasha, her gray eyes wide with fear, storms without knocking into our new quarters, saying one word: *Russki!* We understand, but there is no place here for her or us to hide. The only way out is through the window. The drop from the window sill to the manure pile is only a few meters, and one after the other we make the distasteful jump. Together we run toward the woods, fear speeding us on, and we escape unseen. Much later the women come looking for us to tell us that the dangerous troop has moved on.

Another day we have more time to plan. When the raucous singing and drinking of the Russians promises to last into the night, Mia and Pani confer, for once seeing eye to eye, fearing for our safety. Disguised as "Russian-spooks," with hoes and rakes on our shoulders as if on a purposeful errand, Marianne, Tasha, and I walk before dark to the manor house far from the center of the village and spend the night relatively protected by the Polish administrator of the estate and his contingent of militia.

Thus times of extremes form a common bond between the Polish and German girls—the frivolous days of Konstantin's leave, the fear of Russian molestation. When nothing unusual happens, we go our separate ways.

The Black Way of Life

Winter closes in. Inclement gray days succeed one another in depressing likeness, late dawn hardly lifting from the quiet village before early dusk settles over it again for another long, long night. Bare black branches of trees reach toward the leaden sky, mourning summer's splendor of leaves that rot in soggy brown patches beneath them. Only the evergreens on the slopes thrive as always, but they now seem a remote and darkly threatening enclosure from the world beyond.

In the crowded room over the manure pile, the single small window admits so little daylight, never bright to begin with, that the room remains cloaked in varying shades of gray, reflecting the outside gloom as in a dirty mirror. One lamp from the ceiling lights only the area directly underneath, leaving shadows to shroud the farther reaches and accentuating the darkness that filters in through the window. Even memories of the companionable coziness of such winter evenings in other years are diminished by our sinking spirits. In this small, dim place, the rays of hope and bursts of defiance that occasionally enlivened the preceding months have dwindled as surely as the decreasing light of the year, and our thoughts are as gray and gloomy as the days outside.

Cords are strung over the cooking stove for drying our most indispensable laundry, and for lack of space a few pieces are limply hanging there most of the time, the whites no longer white and the colors fading from lack of proper care. When Eugen comes from his unheated quarters to our room for warmth, he covers his eyes, feigning shock at the display of dingy lingerie.

"Brassieres! Panties! What, no sanitary belts? Such charming diversions you offer to an old man!"

"At least we still wash our underwear," I retort, only half amused.

"My girl, mine is far too precious to ever part with," he says, patting his chest. "Oh, how this padding warms my heart and soul!"

For weeks he has traded most of his own and Egon's zloty wages for German money, which is worthless here. When not working, he goes to outlying farms to offer zloties in exchange at an unrealistic rate for German marks which many Poles have from who knows what sources and are glad to get rid of for money they can use. Sown inside his winter underwear, his wealth is not easily detected and always with him. Visions of once again becoming an independent businessman have sustained him as nothing else could have done.

"Germany, are you ready for an enterprising citizen?" This question is more than facetious to him.

As we become less responsive, his humor grows tired and his attempts at cheerfulness less and less frequent. And then, one morning, he and his son strike out in search of their family and hoped-for new fortune in the west.

We have now taken the grain we had gathered from the empty fields to the mill in a neighboring village in exchange for flour, but its usefulness is limited for lack of other ingredients. When Pani lets us have some milk, we cook a pasty milk and flour soup that is hot and momentarily filling. Potatoes are in ample supply—mashed, boiled, roasted—but seldom seasoned with more than a sprinkle of salt.

The women decide that they must do something to maintain the health of their families because it is bound to suffer from this insufficient diet by spring when the woods and fields will yield fruit again. Money is the key to the modest treasures that are once again available in the stores—foreign money that is inaccessible to us. Before all of us become too weak and dispirited, Aunt Gretl rallies her courage and begins the quest for money. It means parting with yet more of our possessions, mainly clothes, and the clothes that we can most easily spare, because they may never be needed again, are what we still have of her husband's and Father's things.

While the Russians have looted and destroyed belongings indiscriminately, the Poles have pursued confiscation on a grander scale, appropriating real property and whole households, choosing only personal articles that happen to take their fancy and often leaving the rest to the real owners. Once established in their new homes with all necessities and comforts and in possession of money to buy what they want, acquisition becomes for them a game to enjoy. And the best bargains are to be found on the black market, which, though outlawed, thrives openly in the towns. It is a buyers' market because the sellers are parting with their wares almost glad of any value that can still be extracted from them. For the sellers, driven by the need to survive, this method of obtaining money or more often goods in trade is a risky business at best. Any time they remove something of their own from Polish-appropriated premises, they are guilty of theft. Concealment is the next problem—any goods too obviously carried off may simply be taken away without remuneration. Finding an interested trader among all the strangers is hard, and finding a reliable and "honest" black marketeer is hardest of all. And every precarious step throughout the proceedings is a breach of the law. There is no chance in the village to dispose of black goods because word spreads too easily among the resident Poles.

Aunt Gretl goes to town with a pair of men's shoes in her shopping bag. Much to her surprise, people in passing murmur a price for her coat, which she has no intention of selling, and finger her silk scarf, assessing its quality. She feels surrounded by bargain hunters. Encouraged by the ease of making contacts, she enters into the game, offering the shoes until she finds a buyer. The pittance in Polish money which she proudly displays on her return home is enough for a few loaves of bread.

In weeks following she makes more daring ventures into the twilight zone of business, and we eat our way through the smaller items of our men's shrinking wardrobes. But the possessions that promise a more substantial gain are too risky to carry into the street market place.

Aunt Gretl becomes acquainted with a trader who is willing to bid on merchandise unseen and to set up clandestine meetings to conclude a deal. Money seldom changes hands; he prefers to pay in food which, indeed, is the ultimate goal of Aunt Gretl's deals. Eventually, she trusts him enough to hint at the most valuable piece of clothing we have decided to sell—after tearful consultation with Mother, to whom every sale of Father's belongings is like a betrayal of his trust. But anything we cannot or will not sell could be lost without any benefit to any of us, and Mother relents to the desperate need to keep the family better fed.

The black marketeer promises to come to the village to claim his bargain. He arrives in the dusk of a dreary winter evening, full of cheer and bonhomie, towering above us who expect our sacrifice to be duly appreciated. He looks about the desolate room in which we live and tells us not to worry—such is life: To be dancing on top of the table sometimes and crouching in the dirt beneath it at other times; times will change for us again as they have changed for him.

Mother pulls Father's fur coat from under the bed cover where she had hidden it earlier for this occasion, strokes the fluffy lining, caresses the soft collar as if it were a living thing, and watches the man's eyes light up in admiration. No need to feel the Ulster cloth on the outside or test the fur; he can see the quality of material and workmanship. He also knows that we cannot refuse any offer he wants to make, now that the coat is in open view and his for better or worse. The price he pays is a ten-pound bucket of lard.

For supper Aunt Gretl fries a big skillet full of potatoes, and they taste as delicious as they smell. Mother picks at them without appetite.

"What is the matter with you? Why don't you eat?" demands Aunt Gretl with irritation.

"I am just not hungry," is Mother's excuse.

"Stop that foolishness," persists Aunt Gretl without mercy. "Be grateful that we have anything to put on your plate."

Mother sobs: "Did we really have to do it?"

"What? What? You mean selling Josef's coat? A lot of good it would do him or any of us if it were stolen! Hede, don't you understand," Aunt Gretl tries a more soothing approach, "he would understand. He has always taken care of you, and even in this insane way he is still doing it. Go on, eat, you are nothing but skin and bones and wrinkles."

All through the winter Father's fur coat that would never again have shielded him from the raw east wind supplies us with shortening to vary our poor meals. We take comfort in the thought that he would have been the last to deny us sustenance—would truly have given his life to sustain us.

Perils of Friendship

Aunt Gretl and I as her usual accomplice are returning by train from a minor forage trip in town; because of the bitter cold we have spent precious zloties for tickets. The only other passenger left on the platform is a small, middle-aged woman, toting an unwieldy bag and a large suitcase obviously too heavy for her. After a few steps toward the village she deposits her baggage on the pavement and straightens up, looking dejectedly about her. Aunt Gretl offers our help, and together the three of us carry the load more easily. The Polish woman warms to Aunt Gretl's conversation and tells her that she has been to her former home for winter clothes which she had left behind. She bemoans the fact that her upstairs apartment in a farmhouse is cold and that she has not managed to bring along some warm bedding as well. To Aunt Gretl and me, the most remarkable thing about the incident is that the Polish woman is content to live in unsatisfactory quarters and wants to rely on her own resources to make them more livable.

She is not alone in suffering from the discomforts of the cold, snowy weather. Aunt Gretl's friends from her home city, who live in one of the high-ceilinged, chilly rooms of the manor house complain of not keeping warm even in bed. Compared to them, we at the inn are snug in our crowded room, warmed by the cooking stove by day and by our deep, soft featherbeds at night. Since we had to move to our smaller quarters, some of us have to double up in the few beds and don't even need all of the feather covers any more.

Aunt Gretl wants to lend one of them to the two women friends in the manor house. Even tightly rolled, the light bundle is awkward to carry for one person, so I accompany Aunt Gretl on this errand of mercy on an afternoon early enough to allow time to return before nightfall. Our steps on the frozen road are the only sounds under the snow-laden sky. We hurry to get across the bridge and past the village hall at the far end without being seen. Compassionate and innocent though our intention may be, the people at the village hall might question it.

Halfway across the bridge, a man comes running toward us, chased by the radical young mayor brandishing a cane. Forcing ourselves to continue without showing any reaction, we can predict that our errand is over. The rhythm of two sets of steps rushing away from us is broken, one of them receding in the distance, the other reversing itself. Aunt Gretl whispers under her breath:

"Remember the woman at the train station? The bed is for her!"

The Pole with the cane is upon us, cracking it across the soft bundle, hissing questions at us. He marches us to the village hall for interrogation by him and his cohorts. He pushes Aunt Gretl into a room by herself and motions an elderly man in coat and hat to take charge of me. That one grabs me roughly by the arm and pulls me into another room. Adam, the mayor, speaking in Polish seems to explain our offense, pointing accusingly at the evidence, the featherbed on the floor. Aunt Gretl's raised voice from the room across the hall is muffled when the door slams shut. We are to be questioned separately.

The man in the hat has a cane, too; by way of introduction he lets it whistle through the air.

"What is in this bundle?" he demands to know.

"A featherbed," I answer.

"Where did you steal it?"

"It's not stolen," I correct him, "it's ours."

A step to the side and the cane burns across my buttocks.

"Where do you live?" he asks.

"At the inn."

"Don't you know that the inn belongs to K.?" Without waiting for an answer, he slams the cane down on me again.

"Where are you trying to smuggle stolen goods?"

"Nothing is stolen," I insist. "We wanted to give an extra bed to the woman who lives at the farm of X. and needs one."

The cane is out of control and dances up and down my spine.

"How would you know that she needs a bed? How do you even know her?" he probes.

"We met her at the station and talked with her," I reply. Against the poised cane I throw a shielding arm across my back and receive the full blow above my wrist. The man glowers at me in threatening silence, while I bite back tears of panic and pain.

Adam enters, and an excited conversation in Polish ensues between the men in which they are presumably comparing notes. They call out a name and an order, then the front door slams. Interminable minutes of being left standing, while the Poles exchange an occasional remark. Then a man walks in, followed by the woman from the train station. She is clearly puzzled and alarmed by the mayor's summons. They bring in Aunt Gretl whose doleful eyes meet mine.

It is the Polish woman's turn to be questioned. Gestures indicate that she is asked about her acquaintance with the two German offenders. When she obviously answers in the negative, shaking her head, Aunt Gretl and I exchange glances of despair.

"Liars!" A pair of canes comes down on Aunt Gretl and me, but she calls out, undeterred, to remember the heavy baggage we had helped her carry from the station!

"They claim they were taking a bed to you—stolen goods!" The canes land in unison again.

"Stop!" yells the woman in dawning recognition and unstrung by the violence. She recounts the casual meeting and conversation about her cold quarters—she never intended to ask for our help. Aunt Gretl dares reiterate that we never claimed that she did.

The men stand undecided, faced with the testimony of three women that meshes irrefutably. "Figure out women," I read in the uncomprehending shrug of my tormentor. Short of further displaying themselves in the presence of one of their least aggressive compatriots for the brutal men they are, they must desist without any more violence.

Words are their only weapons now, designed to cut the Germans down and apprise them of their rightless status. The corpus delicti remains in the middle of the floor, unfolded and marked by the tips of canes, and the Polish woman on whom we based our only acceptable defense stands embarrassed before the tribunal as Aunt Gretl and I leave the place of our degradation.

We no longer have any doubt of what the future holds for us. We are have-nots and know-nothings. Once again we owe our escape to a deception because truth is a crime we cannot afford to commit, and rights a luxury we cannot claim.

Season to be Jolly

Christmas should not come this year; too great is the irony at this time to celebrate "the feast of peace." To cheer us, Aunt Gretl and Mother have cut a tiny evergreen tree in the woods, which now stands on the table decorated with a single candle.

Aunt Gretl, ever surprising in her temperamental ups and downs, has decided to play Santa Claus for Mia's children, and Mother has fabricated an indefinable stuffed toy out of scraps of material for each of them. Garbed like no *Sankt Nikolaus* we have ever seen, Aunt Gretl returns from Mia's apartment, determined to lift our spirits. She lights the candle and starts singing, prodding us to join her. We go along for a few carols to humor her, but each spreads more nostalgia—it's no use. She tries reminiscing, and almost succeeds with her lively tales, to rescue us from gloom, when Tasha comes to invite all of us to the kitchen. Marianne and I refuse most emphatically.

"We can't insult these people. You two are going with the rest of us," orders her mother.

Pani is waiting for us, beaming goodwill; her husband courteously kisses our hands and motions us around the table. We smile politely and partake of vodka and cookies, indicating to Pani's delight how good they are, and leave as soon as good manners allow.

"They meant to be kind to us. They didn't have to invite us," Mother remarks pointedly to Marianne and me. "Girls, after all, this is Christmas Eve!"

"Where is their Christmas spirit the rest of the time?" I challenge her. "They had Christmas all year long, picking us clean."

"I wish they had left us alone," says Marianne sadly. "I was just beginning to enjoy Mother's yarns."

We go to bed early, and early on Christmas Day I meet Heia to hear once more the glorious music of Christmas resound in the church of my hometown.

Marianne is upset when I return. Aunt Gretl had all but promised to make a trip to Breslau. A few times in the fall they had gone there, first to find what was left of their home and who of their friends, and later to take advantage of the flagrantly conducted black market. During the siege of Breslau, an area large enough to land planes had been leveled near the center of the city for air-lifting troops and supplies. This spacious expanse amid the rubble had become an open-air market place, and in spite of prohibition against black marketeering few people obeyed or were deterred by perfunctory raids, which, at worst, meant to have one's wares confiscated.

In the course of their trips, Aunt Gretl and Marianne have located some old friends and have become acquainted with a few Poles who treat them like friends, and typically for her, Marianne has formed some tender bonds. From the one trip on which I accompanied them, the most abiding memory was a balalaika-playing young Pole. His music, more than his person, had an entrancing effect on me.

Now Aunt Gretl has decided to renege on this trip to Breslau.

"The train fare isn't all that expensive," she admits. "But what little money we have may have to last a long time. Honestly, my nerves aren't up to it—that city holds too many memories for me."

"For me, too, Mother. But you know how alive I feel there even now! We have been cooped up in this misery until I can't bear it, and now you ruin the only thing I have looked forward to," complains Marianne.

"Feel alive!" mocks Aunt Gretl. "You are lucky to be alive, there or anywhere."

"If you won't go, Gina can go with me," she looks at me entreatingly, "and if we go during the holidays, Annemie may be able to go along."

They argue back and forth. Marianne tries another tack.

"Mother, this is Christmas!" she pleads. "Please, for my Christmas present, please, let me go! We could stay at Miss R.'s and be back in two or three days. It may be the last time if the Poles really intend to throw us out."

"In God's or the devil's name go, then, if the others are fools enough to go with you."

Marianne hugs her mother. Her elation is such that I don't want to spoil it for her, and before Aunt Gretl has a chance to change her mind, we persuade my sister to come along. All we need is a confirmation from Miss R., and since the mail service has improved much in recent months, we do not have long to wait.

A few days later we are happily welcomed by Aunt Gretl's friend. Among her first words to Marianne are:

"Adam can hardly wait to see you. He has a big apartment upstairs, as you know; he says there is plenty of room for all of you." She dotes on the Polish student and, obviously, has no qualms about his offer.

"Aren't you glad you came?" Marianne smiles at me. "Adam can play the balalaika for you."

Adam is every bit as charming as I remember him. He turns the apartment over to us, opens his kitchen cabinets to show that he is well supplied, and teases that he expects a good dinner for all of us that evening.

Alex, a friend of his, drops by and stays as late as the curfew will allow. Both young men speak German well enough for coherent conversation, and we talk and laugh and, best of all, listen to Adam playing his balalaika. This promises to be fun! Adam's schedule is such that we have the apartment to ourselves most of the time. Next afternoon Miss R. goes with us to the black market that is as crowded and lively as expected.

While she and I haggle with someone over an article she is selling, we lose sight of Marianne and Annemie. We spot them being pushed into a streetcar by a militia officer. Miss R. screams "Marianne!" and I run after them, but the streetcar has pulled away.

To reassure me and herself, Miss R. reminds me that people are often picked up for short-time work assignments or to have their papers checked, just as I know from Glatz. Marianne knows the city well, although orientation is made difficult by the destruction, and wherever they have been taken, we trust that they will make their way back at the first opportunity. There is nothing for us to do but go home and wait.

Adam and Alex are at the apartment and, hearing of the incident, offer the same explanation. They each bury their nose in a textbook, and I read a history book that I have brought with me, praying for the doorbell to ring. Alex, who had singled me out for special attention on the previous evening, gives up studying and engages me in a debate about history, theirs and ours—how different they are with regards to some of the same events! There is an intensity about him that makes me uncomfortable, and he exhibits a streak of sarcasm compared to which mine is barely discernible. But he is intelligent and knowledgeable.

It has been hours since Marianne and Annemie disappeared. I can no longer control my worry, and Adam, too, becomes apprehensive. He decides to go off on his bicycle to make an inquiry at the nearest militia station.

"Let him take care of it," demands Alex after Adam leaves. "You concentrate on me," and he continues our conversation.

"Enough of history! What else do you know? How is your Latin?"

I spout a few remembered passages, feeling on safe ground, adding lightly:

"How is yours? See if you can make any sense of this! But it only works in German," and I begin to recite a nonsense phrase: "*Unus ignis quis vir multum ab audire . . .*"

"How about this?" he asks. "*Inter pedes puellarum est voluptas puerorum.*" With that, he smothers me in a fierce embrace that leaves me gasping and kisses me with such passion that I go limp with fright. Misinterpreting, he tries to carry me to the couch, but I kick and struggle to free myself.

"Have you gone mad?" I shout at him.

"Yes, mad over you." He lunges toward me as I try to circle around him toward the door and holds my shoulders in a grip that hurts.

"What do you have against me?" he asks seriously and more calmly.

"Nothing. I hardly know you, and I don't like being attacked by strange men."

As long as he holds me at arm's length, I am willing to discuss even this subject with him. But Adam's return forestalls any further exchanges. As if a mask were falling over his face, Alex reverts to a cool formality. By Adam's expression we can see that he brings no good news—he brings no news at all.

Alex leaves soon afterwards. I am in no condition to tempt fate and spend the night at Miss R.'s.

Next morning, Adam, Miss R., and I make the rounds of several militia stations, with Adam as spokesman, while she and I wait outside. His obvious concern increases my worry. What can we do? We return to the apartment house at a loss what to do next.

Marianne and Annemie sit in the apartment, worrying where everyone else is, while we were out searching for them.

"Where have you been?" we ask each other.

"Are you all right?" Adam and I hug them with relief.

"What happened?"

"This militia officer and two civilians demanded to see our papers and took us to the German mayor. There was nothing wrong with our papers! Then the officer made us clean his apartment that was near the mayor's office and promised to let us go afterwards. Of course, he was lying! He insisted on demonstrating a fancy radio to us, and by that time it was getting dark. Then he was going to take us to the streetcar, he lied again, and instead took us to a 'prima' colleague of his who was having a party—no less, the city commandant! I think I am getting sick," moans Marianne.

"On the way I thought we had had it," shudders Annemie. "We heard someone shout '*Stoi!*'—who would not stop when a Russian yells '*Stoi!*' Do you know what that crazy man did? He turned around, linking arms with both of us, pulled out his pistol and kept walking. Backwards!"

"Don't even talk about it! I want to go to sleep, and when I wake up, try to think it was a nightmare."

They sleep most of the day. Later Marianne confesses to me that they, undoubtedly, had spent the worst night of their lives, fighting off drunken guests and not knowing how successfully.

"Don't you think we ought to go home?" I suggest. "I am ready."

"We can't. They would want to know why. We will go tomorrow as if nothing had happened. Don't breathe a word of it!"

In the evening we sit down together as on the first one— we have cause to celebrate—but the carefree companionship is somehow lacking. Too much has happened to each of us. Alex delays leaving until it is too late and has to stay.

As before, I make my bed on the living-room couch. When I think that everyone is quiet and properly bedded, Adam comes and sits down by me.

"You see, they came back safely. They had a bad scare—we all did," he says soothingly, caressing my face. But suddenly he is lying next to me and touches me as no one has ever touched me before, and I see a dark shadow looming in the dark over me: Alex, with a gun in his hand.

"*Er oder ich?*" he hisses.

Him or me? Him or me? reverberates in my head. Which of us will you shoot?

He and Adam start arguing furiously in Polish. Suddenly both are gone, and no shot has fallen. I dare not move. When I wake up, I am not alone on the couch. Someone is holding my hand. Next to me, fully dressed, lies Alex, looking at me. When he sees the panic in my eyes, he kisses my forehead and leaves without saying a word.

Reason returns with the morning light. We prepare breakfast and pack our bags.

"What was the commotion about last night after we went to bed?" whispers Marianne.

"Some argument," I whisper back. "Nothing has happened. Tell you later." Nothing had happened, and suddenly I know what Adam had told his murder-minded friend and what had turned Alex's demon into a lamb. My innocence had prevailed against them.

Adam walks us to the train station and sends regards to Aunt Gretl. We talk little on the way home.

Illness

Sworn to secrecy, we dwell in uncalled-for breadth on the bright, or at least inoffensive, events of our Breslau adventure, hoping that these will be accepted as plausible explanation of how we spent the two terrible days. But our minds are occupied with the unspoken, unspeakable ones. Annemie must cope with them as best she can away from us; Marianne and I have each other to talk to in unguarded moments.

"I break out in cold sweat at night, recalling the commandant's arrogant voice: 'How dare you resist me! Don't you know who I am?' He showed me what he was—an animal! Oh, my God, why did this have to happen to me?" she wails. She talks of suicide. She won't eat.

Blaming part of her problems on her flashy blond hair, she dyes it brunette with some shelf-aged remedy from the village store. When she can't stand her new mirror image and tries to wash it out, it dries to a greenish cast.

"I was trying to be good," she weeps. "And now God is striking me with ugliness."

We sink into a depression deeper than the one before Christmas. Although I want to dismiss our fall from grace as past and done with, I smart with my new, disillusioned knowledge of the world. Gnawing still on my mind as well is the memory of the beating by the Poles; the welts have long receded from my body, but invisible scars remain.

Although my upbringing had been strict, corporeal punishment was considered the lowest, most uncivilized form of discipline, as shameful to the one who deals it out as to the one who receives it, and was rarely resorted to. To become its victim unjustly at the hands of power-crazed strangers is even more reprehensible, and life under the rule of such brutes intolerable.

Inactive winter days leave too much time for brooding. Added to the two shattering experiences, the unbearable frustrations of the last, lost year prey constantly on my mind. With the irrationality of despair, I am gripped by an insatiable hunger for the youth I have been denied, for the kind of life I had expected to enjoy, and withdrawing into myself, I create a glittering fantasy world of romantic illusions where every day is brilliant with sunshine and every night a star-studded miracle, and where the imagined greatest love of all time waits to fill me with ecstasy beyond mundane comprehension. To empty the cup of life in one greedy gulp, to beg of the fleeting moment: "*Verbleibe doch, du bist so schön!*" and tumble from the intoxication with life into death . . .

The more turbulent my secret life, the more resigned I appear on the surface, and I move through the days like an automaton. Giving in to my growing physical lassitude, I refuse to leave bed one morning. Mother watches me more closely and detects an ominous yellow cast underneath my pallor. She forces me to get dressed and take the next train to town in search of a doctor.

Whatever ails me is not something he can diagnose without laboratory tests, but he has no facilities for these. Complete bed rest and control of the as yet low-grade fever is the best he can advise.

I sleep or doze constantly, hardly touching what food Mother tries to force on me. My fantasies slip from my control into fever dreams.

. . . Spring! What glorious warmth floods my cheeks! The birches seem transparent with the breath of new leaves floating about them. I know well and love this path along the tracks near Wartha. In a few minutes I will reach the railroad station. I should see it soon.

Where is the station?

Where now are the birches that lead to it? These trees are too dark—the light is fading. I must find the train! These tracks beside me must lead me to it.

Run before night falls—run to get home!

Light shines where the woods end, run for it!

I AM running as fast as I can—my pulse is hammering—I can't breathe—I can't see!

Light, where have you gone? Where is the path?

I am lost, LOST—I have never been here before! The trees are reaching for me. Oh no, don't hold me! Let me go home . . .

Fighting against the weight that threatens to crush me, I suddenly feel something light and cool touching my forehead. Mother's troubled eyes swim into focus dimly. I am no longer lost but very, very weak from the poison of fever. Mother bathes me with cool, soft cloths until I drift into gentle slumber.

. . . The essay turned out well. I can always think best in the dining room behind closed doors, and the gentle sounds and air of spring through the open windows make me feel like singing—so happy—so alive. Now I can start copying my masterpiece to make it look as neat as it is good. There is no hurry.

The first page is perfect, every letter, every comma, as it should be. My hand has caught the rhythm of my mind and moves smoothly over the paper.

Slowly, slowly, I say, no slipping below the line.

Dash it, the letters are getting sloppy! That squiggle shouldn't be there at all. The pen, it's the pen! It yanks my hand up and down and I can't let go of it!

The letters are bigger than three lines now—no words any more—just furious zigzags! A crazy circle is growing bigger and bigger—my whole arm is going wild with it! The page is tearing. Why can't I stop?

Oh, my paper, my beautiful paper . . .

I wake to my own sobbing and grip the steady hand that is taking my pulse. My own other hand is clenched so hard that the nails bite into the palm. How can I finish my paper now, I think, still confused by the dream. A soothing voice tells me that I will be fine when the fever stays down, and the cool compresses will refresh me. Yes, that is better. Grateful and tired, I relax and sleep again.

. . . Spring, and the lilacs are in bloom. I close my eyes and drink in the fragrance, breathing deeply. I want to fill my lungs with the perfume of lilacs until it pervades my whole being. My head sinks toward the blossoms, hungering for more, inhaling the sweetness in great gulps. Faster, faster before they wilt and rot!

I look at the blossoms bursting with life and beauty; they are all about me, and I want to drain them of all their scent. My breath is so powerful that it pulls them from the stem. I can't stop sucking and slurping. They fill my mouth—my throat is full of them.

The lilacs are invading me! The smell is going to my head. I am dizzy—I need air . . .

And I lie panting, my tongue curled thick and dry against my throat. In the dim light I recognize a glass of water by the bedside and reach for it unsteadily to wash the choking from my throat. It shatters on the floor and brings Mother running in alarm.

At last the fever subsides, and I lie weak and wide awake, tired unto death, so tired that the thought of having to stay alive makes me weep quietly into my pillow. Once two Russian soldiers walk into our room. Aunt Gretl, with a mournful voice and pointing in my direction, says only one word:

"*Kaputt!*"

They glance at me and quickly withdraw from possible contamination. Thus introduced into the real world from which I had escaped into fever and nightmares, I get angry at being tossed back into the senseless vegetation that our existence has become. My pulse now begins pounding from irritation, and I want it to be the first sign of sinking into a relapse. But my body rallies against my wishes, the fever does not recur, the jaundice is fading, and I rejoin the others, a shaky replica of myself. While recovering from one illness, I am sickened through and through by another one, by the insanity I refuse to call life.

Calendar of Final Days

Wednesday, February 20, 1946

On this fateful date the compulsory evacuation of Germans in Lower Silesia is set in motion. How long have we been afraid, hoping against hope that this day would never come, yet waiting all the time for some momentous event to release us from intolerable conditions? Of all possible solutions this is the most deeply feared and bitterly resented. For months it had been rumored; and yet, when it actually happens, it strikes as devastating a blow as awareness of imminent death after a long, lingering illness. We are too stunned to grasp the enormity of the bereavement that is upon us. We stand numb before the bankruptcy, our own and that of generations before us. They had made this land ours by their sweat and blood. How can a whole people be uprooted, disowned, tossed aside like useless flotsam—how? With the stroke of a pen, with a new line drawn on a map, we are sentenced to homelessness.

Politics is the continuation of war by other means, I think bitterly, rephrasing von Clausewitz, who claimed that war was the continuation of politics by other means.

The lethargy of the winter months gives way to an almost relieving excitement, a tension without sorrow or fear that is exhausting and enlivening at the same time. A stressful waiting begins. We wait without knowing what we are waiting for; what lies ahead is without parallel in our experience.

Two of Konstantin's friends who are visiting the Polish family occupy an upstairs room. They are friendly young men who like to spend as much time with us as with their hosts. Now they take it upon themselves to break with encouraging words the paralyzing spell that grips us. We are only too grateful and eager to receive some matter-of-fact assurance that no harm will come to us: Whatever happens now, they explain, is no longer willful vengeance of individuals against individuals but an orderly procedure directed by international authority. Somehow the dread of chaos and abuse is allayed and transformed into a sad and resigned anticipation of the inevitable moment of departure.

The approach of the zero hour holds for me a special terror that I am hiding from the others. A messenger from the manor house has delivered a note from Annemie to me. At the advice of some influential acquaintance, she has decided to stay here until the initial commotion is over and to leave for the west voluntarily later with that man's family. Mother assumes, of course, that she will be expelled with the Germans from the manor house and join us on the mass transport. What shall I do? How can she lay this burden on me? Can I risk losing her, my only remaining blood kin, and bear the guilt for the rest of my life? But what have I to offer to persuade her to come along with us? No one knows where we will go and what will happen to us; she may be the only one to escape from a worse fate than we have known so far. Once I demanded a pistol to hold the choice of life or death in my own hands. I cannot deny her the right to this choice now. I must keep silent.

We pack our suitcases and backpacks more discriminately than we ever packed before because we know that anything that cannot be fitted into our hand baggage will be lost to us forever. Suddenly the woeful cry of all refugees—We lost everything!—comes back to haunt us; we still have much more than we can carry, and the agonizing selection among our remaining belongings is harder to face than random theft and destruction by an enemy.

The grim winter weather becomes an unexpected ally. Each of us stages a private dress rehearsal of how to slip layer over layer of clothing that can be worn instead of packed. Against the dreaded uncertainty of where our means of support will come from to launch us into a new life, we sew pockets into underwear to hide what German currency we still have, just as Eugen had done. We must keep faith in our ultimate destination at this time when no one knows whether we are bound for the west and deliverance or east toward a fate too bleak to imagine.

By nightfall, we are exhausted and plagued by doubts whether we have chosen well or forgotten essentials we will miss later.

Thursday, February 21, 1946

A neighboring village is on the move. Surely, our time is only hours away. Hours of tense idleness, listening for strange voices to give a signal—what signal, what clue? Waiting is torture.

Friday, February 22, 1946

From the moment of awakening, alertness tightens every muscle and stretches every nerve. Again nothing happens, and the room that has become an obstacle course of pieces of baggage and the multiple layers of clothing we wear are too confining to endure for yet another day of endless hours of waiting. The continuing quiet makes our readiness seem premature and ridiculous.

Marianne and I are the first to surrender to the urge to break through the senseless tension; we peel off unnecessary dresses and, clothed in normal wraps, we set out to visit the elderly couple from Berlin to relax ourselves as well as our friends. Like prisoners unshackled we relish the walk on the deserted road and breeze into our friends' *tristesse* a happy surprise. The old people have also packed, but there is so little they feel strong enough to carry with them that their room seems unchanged and much more comfortable than the crowded storage room left behind at the inn. The visit is such a relief that the thought of farewell mercifully stays hidden in secret recesses of our minds.

But all too soon reality intrudes again in the person of Aunt Gretl, who breathlessly fetches us home because evacuation is scheduled for 8:00 P.M.—and none of us questions the authoritativeness of her announcement. Upon our return to the inn, the young Poles' serious miens seem to confirm the rumors of imminent departure.

Eight o'clock passes—the strain changes to resentment. We feel too much on edge to be lulled into security or risk getting ready for the night.

The Polish visitors' room receives us into pleasant warmth, soft light, and the strains of radio music. Our own room next door belongs to another world that is easy to forget, even for a few minutes. The young Poles treat us to vodka and cigarettes, making us feel like welcome guests, and the tension gradually melts away. An evening ensues like a few others before, when together we listened to broadcasts in a variety of languages, translating for one another, and talked in civil conversation like equals and friends, and under the watchful eyes of Mother and Aunt Gretl even dared indulge in harmless flirtation. Minutes can thus glide into hours unnoticed. The women stifle a yawn now and then but do not want to disturb the pleasant diversion that brings a little sparkle to our eyes and revives the illusion of youth.

On this evening more than any other, when our fate lies hidden under so many unanswered questions, we open ourselves to the soft night music—the sentimental popular tunes of recent years that know no bounds of nationality, each throbbing with the smooth rhythm of graceful dance movement and blurring the line between past and present. This is not the time or place for dancing, but the feeling of dance, of being close in rhythmic harmony, swings in the room. I dreamily remember the sweet-sad ups and downs of inconsequential past crushes on boys who had to become men before their time—men I will never know; and I am no longer the love-struck girl who learned to dance foxtrot and tango and whirled breathlessly to waltz after waltz. Only the melodies of those days remain, and most of them are sad and lonely.

. . . J'attendrai—le jour et la nuit
j'attendrai toujours
ton retour . . .

J'attendrai—I will wait. Everybody is waiting, everywhere, all the time.

Saturday, February 23, 1946

It is time to go. The Iron Cross next door that had spewed the last German combat soldiers into the hands of the arriving Russians has been designated as the gathering station for our section of the village. Pani embraces each of her departing housemates tearfully and bids us farewell in words we cannot understand.

In the public rooms of the Iron Cross we sit on and in the midst of all we own and wait from early morning. Once in the building, no German is allowed to leave. At noon Tasha and her little brother bring hot, thick potato soup and a pitcher of milk.

By 3:00 P.M. the doors are opened, and we are told to go home. Pani's startled and puzzled look makes the reunion after that morning's emotional good-bye an embarrassment because no one is prepared to resume an awkward relationship.

We carry our bags back to the depressing abandoned room, and after days of dismantling and packing decide to make the place more livable again, preparing for a less stressful wait of days, even weeks—who can say how long? Discounting the abortive evacuation attempt as a typical example of Polish inefficiency, we rather smugly hang up our clothes before calmly settling down for the night.

Sunday, February 24, 1946

The illusion does not last through the night. A hard knock on the door before daybreak is accompanied by the terse order to be ready in ten minutes. We feel no panic, just cold fury which clears the sleep-sodden heads and speeds every motion to a machinelike precision.

We are at the bottom of the stairs, ready to leave the house.

"Listen to me," announces Aunt Gretl, highly agitated. "We are not going—not now and not like this. I won't be driven from my father's house."

Before we can assimilate what she has said, she collapses on the flag-stoned hall, staging a very convincing heart attack. We hover above her, speechless and in apparent concern for her, without having to pretend. I wonder if, in truth, she has finally lost her mind. Pani rushes to her aid with medication which the "patient" refuses weakly, indicating by a motion of her hand that takes in all of us that we must go back upstairs and carry her to bed.

Pani loses her composure and runs to the barn for her husband. He rushes to the Iron Cross for advice on how to cope with the distressing incident. Aunt Gretl still leans propped up against the steps with a tormented expression on her face. The Polish farmer returns and makes us understand that we need not leave: Aunt Gretl has won a reprieve for us.

Meanwhile the people assembled at the Iron Cross are filing outside, one burdened evacuee after another, and slowly a sad procession begins to move across the bridge. The truth of what is happening, that we alone will be left behind, turns Aunt Gretl's heart attack into a cruel joke on herself.

"What am I doing to you," she mumbles to herself. "All of our people will be gone, and we the only ones left among strangers." The struggle that tears her apart—wanting to stay in her father's house and wanting to go with the villagers—marks her face with naked anguish. When the commotion of the departing trek dies down, she truly panics:

"Go, go, we must go! Hurry to catch up with them!"

The decision revives her from both her pretended and real spell, and we reach for our baggage. The farewells remain unsaid this time, but at the last moment, one of the young men who had befriended us holds back Marianne and vows to find her wherever she will be taken.

We stragglers hurry from the inn to the village hall, the same house in which Aunt Gretl and I suffered the beating. There are no formalities to rescind our less than hour-old permission to remain since neither agreement is dignified by a written document.

The very man whose cane bruised my back so brutally provides a helping hand to speed us on our way—and why not, we are undesirables to be gotten rid of—and carries two of our bags. Along the way he hails a passing farmer to press his cart into temporary service. Despite the source, we are grateful for this unexpected relief, whatever its motivation.

Before we reach the edge of the village, we have caught up to the rear of the trek and melt into the homeless throng. As far as we can see, a ragged line of slowly moving figures hugs one side of the road, urged on by militiamen when someone pauses too long to shift the heavy baggage. Despite the cold we perspire under the overabundance of clothing. The distance to town seems to grow longer and ever more taxing as we plod on. When we passed this way in the opposite direction months ago, not in our most pessimistic apprehensions would we have guessed that our homecoming to town might be the final farewell.

As the procession winds through the streets of town, the most ironic of all coincidences begins to take shape in our minds before the fact confirms it: Our immediate destination is the building complex where our apartment was located, my home of happier times and the place where I faced the grossest wanton lust for destruction.

The large rooms and wide halls of the office wing are completely bare of all furniture. They fill up rapidly as the straggling procession telescopes into a scurrying mass of people, seeking to stake out a few square feet walled in by their baggage. Once settled in family groups, they seem drained of all will and anxious curiosity about the next phase; movement ceases and few have anything to say. For us, even the desire to explore the once familiar building, let alone the place we called home, is stifled by numb resignation. Bedded on the floor fully clothed, we spend a long, wakeful, silent night.

Monday, February 25, 1946

The paved drive and the lawn in front of the building are teeming with evacuees. The ornamental wrought-iron gate is still closed, guarded by armed militia. Soldiers circle the crowd like sheep dogs, trying to force the mass into a manageable shape. When the gate opens, we are sluiced into the street in an orderly stream of three abreast, as orderly as moving mountains of bundles can be grouped. Soldiers patrol the procession on both sides and lead the way to the main station.

Neither afraid nor sad, I feel something like awe well up in me at the momentous events that have flung me into this gray line that crawls faceless, nameless, homeless through my hometown. With a resurgence of identity that being in this mass threatens to deny me, I see myself a minute but individual part of history in the making, and I take each step consciously as if on a pilgrimage over hallowed ground.

We are only minutes from the station when I become aware of a little person scurrying past on the sidewalk. I call a name which my lips have formed countless times with every nuance of joy and distress. Heia's eyes light up in her worried, wrinkled face, and she falls in step beside me, pushing a bag of sandwiches under my arm before the guard roughly gestures her away.

"Little one, I will pray for you," wails Heia as she stands back, disconsolately wringing her hands.

190

"Remember the Bavarian address," is my last cry to link us together beyond this bitter moment. When I look back once more, the beloved figure is still rooted to the spot where the soldier halted her, motionless, gray, forlorn.

The Train

The train stands ready, sliding doors gaping to receive us into the dark space of the freight cars. It seems to stretch for miles beyond the platform, and many of the cars are already occupied. The revulsion of having to clamber up and into the inhospitable black holes is given short shrift by the militia swarming among the evacuees and counting heads to fill each car to capacity. Straw is pushed to the walls around the cavernous rectangle. When the quota in our car is filled, we are told to spread out the straw. Baggage stacked against the walls, each family builds a lair of sorts, and the lucky ones garner a corner as far away from the door and the cold as possible.

Then the platform is empty, except for the militiamen on guard. At a signal the sliding doors clang shut and are latched from the outside. A tiny patch of daylight is visible through an opening set high in the center of one side of the freight car. When the train jerks into motion, we still do not know where it will carry us. The clock on the station building, as we pass it, shows 3:25 P.M. It is Monday, February 25, 1946.

The small window draws me like a magnet. Stepping over bags and around huddled or sprawling bodies, I make my way to it to stand by it as long as the train keeps rolling to see the familiar scenes glide by for the last time. My contact with the world outside is reduced to this square foot of icy exposure; it is better than the dark desolation behind my back. As long as I can see by the passing landmarks where we are going, I cling to this small certainty against the appalling uncertainty of our destination.

The tracks wind away from town toward the mountain

pass, and sometimes bare branches of trees seem close enough to grasp. The birches along this stretch of railroad where I loved to walk in the spring blend their spotted white stems into the sad, gray sky, their frail, stripped limbs drawn like fine lines against it.

The train slows through the town of Wartha, the shrine of the Blessed Virgin with its twin spires majestically outlined against the wooded slopes. There pilgrims from far and near did penance in prayerful procession, as they climbed from station to station of the cross to the summit of Golgotha. And opposite lies a smaller hill, the Rosary Mountain, studded with thirty chapels, one for each secret of the rosary. How many times I have followed each path, less with piety than growing frustration in my childhood, anxious to be done with the prayers and to be turned loose among the booths with souvenirs and the delicious pastries that were a re- nowned specialty, or to roam in the galleries where testi- monials and works of art cover the walls to commemorate miraculous cures.

Leaving Wartha, the train moves away from the moun- tains. Turning to face backwards, I keep them in view—the beautiful mountains that cradle my home—until they fade into a dim line on the horizon. The gently hilly terrain tapers off into the plain, and the train gathers speed. When it passes the castle of Kamenz, I hardly recognize the once stately struc- ture set on a rise in the vast park; it is a burned-out shell, and the pole on which the Hohenzollern flag used to be hoisted to announce the presence of the old prince points an empty, ac- cusing finger from the ruin.

The brakes shriek, bringing the long train to a shudder- ing halt in the Kamenz station, a few kilometers northeast of Glatz. Three years ago—three years or three lifetimes?—an- other train stood here; in it was Gerhard on his way to Russia and death. The brief note he posted from here, so close to home, almost within reach of the mountains he longed to see, was a tortured homesick cry that made us ache with compas- sion for him who rarely betrayed his secret sentimental soul. I know what he must have felt at that moment. Now I, too, am barred from the little paradise beyond the mountains, from home, and even from Mama's grave that lies below the castle within walking distance from the station.

When the doleful journey continues, I stare blindly into the fading light of day. So this is how it feels to be stripped of everything, to be exiled without recourse. I have nothing. I am nothing. I have lost all I loved, all I knew—my family, my friends, my home, and now my country. Why am I alive when I have died piecemeal over and over with each of their deaths, with each farewell, why? Just once more to sit on Father's lap, to hear Franz call me by a pet name, to share a joke with Gerhard—gladly would I trade my whole future for one of these irretrievable moments. Will I ever see strong-headed little Annemie again? My faithful Heia? Will I ever again stand at Mama's grave? I can't bear leaving the scenes that bear their mark. I can't bear it, I can't bear it—the rhythm of the clattering wheels echoes in the desolation of my soul.

By 9:00 P.M. we have been shunted on a side track outside the Breslau station for a long delay. From the opening in the wagon wall, we take turns peering out on dimly lit streets bordered by blocks of ruins. Somewhere in the outskirts beyond the ravaged provincial capital stands Aunt Gretl's home; somewhere out there lie the scenes of carefree childhood days buried under the rubble; somewhere in the livable remnants of the city we broke with childhood.

The night is an ordeal of many restless bodies tossing on the insufficient bed of straw, amidst moans and mutterings of the sleepless and sonorous snores of a few fortunate ones. Each of us is an island of unhappiness in the sea of common misery. As we grow warm in our tightly wedged group, a revolting suspicion of vermin in the straw turns mere discomfort into helpless disgust. Is there no end to degradation even now?

Daylight at last, and more long hours in the inhospitable station. When the train moves again, we should know which way fate has decided we will go. The suspense of waiting for this moment of truth overshadows every thought, with every moment bringing us closer to the revelation which we dread and long for at the same time. Occasionally, the wait is interrupted by a group visit to latrines under armed guard, and the walk through the fresh air is in itself a marvelous relief. When the square-capped soldiers test the latches on the sliding doors, we come alive with anticipation. Locked in once more, we are soon in shuddering motion. The gruesome suspense lasts through innumerable switching maneuvers before the train gains the open track, heading unmistakably in a westerly direction. For the first time we dare hope that, as the young Poles had promised, we will be out of harm's reach. I take up my post by the opening again and call out the names of the stations we pass.

Under the sun-drenched, pale winter sky lies a secluded manor house, a fairy-tale castle in a charmed vale of dreams. Distance produces an illusion of perfection although a closer view might reveal a mere shell. And then comes the vast, lonely plain of pine woods and stretches of sandy barrenness in which isolated settlements in ruins show the horrible wounds of war. Is this still the land I love, this desolation deserted by all signs of human life?

The rhythm of the rolling wheels moves through me with the pulse beat of unspeakable pain. An icy draft stings my eyes as they strain into the dusk until the land that gave birth to all of my dreams—and saw them die—recedes into the gathering darkness as though it had never been.

Epilogue

The travels of the mind that have taken me once again through the war-torn years of my growing up merge into our present trip as if the intervening lifetime were something I had read about in someone else's book. Seeing the East German uniforms, at a glance indistinguishable from those worn by the German soldiers in World War II, bridges the gap uncannily. The unpleasant border incident infuses an element of danger and fear unlike any I have experienced since I left Silesia as a teenager, a fitting link across the years. Was coming back a mistake after all? Again, as I had thought many times while reliving and recording the war and postwar events, I find myself thinking: No one should have to pass that way twice, and never by choice. But just as those stories, once begun, had generated a life of their own and been swept on by their own momentum, there is no turning back for me now.

The dark and silence in the van have left each of us alone with our reflections. I force myself back to the reality of our journey. The roads should become familiar, but the night and the foreign names of the communities through which we pass continue to confuse me.

I ask Hans: "Where are we? I know I have been here before."

"Of course, you have. We are already in Frankenstein."

My homecoming begins where Franz's life had ended. We pass through narrow streets between blocks of tall buildings, now mere shadows and outlines. From here I could take the wheel and without help drive the rest of the way to our destination, Hans's native village. Now I strain to recognize landmarks. Even in the dark I can identify in the next community the imposing shape of a villa once owned by Mama's relatives. Vacations spent there were glorious adventures by day and fearful moments before going to sleep at night, when only Franz's hand across the bedroom aisle reassured me against a long-dead nobleman's ghost. Even in its shadowy existence the haunted house looms as large as in memory.

The roads are narrow now, and only the initiated would find the correct turns through the rural area at night. Now and then the headlights briefly illuminate a building or a corner that I have seen many times before. They brush over the squat two-story home of Helene and Hans, touch the church in the center of the village, then pierce the black side road by the rectory, and the motor dies. We have arrived and are anxious to unfold our limbs and stretch them on waiting beds.

The rectory is dark, save for a lone high window in the rear. Hans leaves to announce our arrival. With the others I step from the van to move about and taste the fresh night air.

"It still smells like your village," I tell Helene, who is restlessly groping around on the dark path. From somewhere music and voices drift toward us, foreign sounds in a night that seems like others long ago.

Across the road the village church rises like a darker shadow against the night sky. Beside us the rectory stands massive and silent, keeping Hans a prisoner. Separately and alone with our thoughts we pace a few steps from the van and back again, only the boys venture with flashlights through the night and announce the discovery of a cemetery at the end of the path. The black sky is speckled with few stars and seems to envelop us down below in its trailing impenetrable train. Helga, for whom this place would have been unfamiliar even in the old days and who lacks any nostalgic attachment to it, has curled up in the van to await the next phase in comfort.

Without Hans we are like a ship without its captain. Even knowing where he is does not dispel a growing feeling of unease because he is gone inordinately long. The minutes of waiting add up to more than half an hour before we hear steps crunching toward us from the gate of the rectory garden. In an uncharacteristically subdued voice Hans mumbles something about a problem when the flashlight picks out his shape and that of the pastor.

The letter announcing our arrival had not reached our would-be host, and on this of all nights he has promised his empty rooms to guests who are attending the wedding of his housekeeper's daughter in the village. Frantic telephone calls to surrounding towns have been unsuccessful. The boys talk excitedly about camping out—they came prepared with a tent, sleeping bags, and air mattresses—the rest of us have unpleasant visions of reclining in the van until morning as best we can.

The pastor holds out a slim hope for a room at a be-friended farmer's house. He steps into the van with us to guide Hans down a long, dark, bumpy lane into a farmyard. The men enter the house while we wait in half-hearted antic-ipation. When the yard light flashes on and three men appear in the doorway, our hopes brighten, too, and Hans's relieved expression reaches us before his words:

"We are staying here at least for tonight."

The pastor stands aside, talking to a middle-aged, un-shaven stranger in a rumpled gray flannel shirt, open-necked and sleeves rolled up, who smiles with amusement as one after another steps stiffly from the van. He greets the boys with a handshake and gallantly kisses the hands of the women.

Loaded with bags and sleeping gear, we invade the house through a dark, flagstoned hall and file into a large, low-ceilinged kitchen lit by a single lamp in the far corner over the table. Immediately to the left of the door, in the darkest cor-ner of the room, stands a bed of sorts on which somebody appears to be sleeping. Several people scurry about and nod to us shyly when the man whose name is Jerzy ushers us into a small room beyond the kitchen, where cards and glasses on the table bear witness to the companionable Saturday night entertainment that our unscheduled arrival has interrupted. And beyond this room lies our haven for the night, a spacious bedroom with a pair of twin beds and a couch, a wardrobe and a dresser, and ample floor space for three air mattresses. Jerzy our host is everywhere, talking to us in laborious German, calling out to the others in Polish, sure and cheerful. Hans takes the pastor home, and by the time he returns from the rectory, we are settled around the table from which the remnants of the card game have been removed and we respond to Jerzy's welcoming toast of straight vodka from the crystal glasses that had graced the cupboard at our arrival.

While two women flutter in and out with fresh bedding, bring plates of bread and meat and relishes, pitchers of juice and glasses of hot tea, we get acquainted with Jerzy and like him instantly. Gratitude has but a small part in our intuitive feeling for him. He seems to know the village well and can identify properties by the names of their former German owners and the new Polish settlers. Anna and Helene are full of questions, and he answers them without embarrassment and with a kind word about many who, like us, came to visit the places they once called home, and there is no rancor in what he says about events beyond his and our control. The vodka limbers his tongue in our language and soothes our weariness and tension. Midnight finds us laughing together at the day's adventures and the good fortune that brought us to his humble home. We feel in good hands and good company.

Before bedtime we are offered a bowl of water that one of the women has heated on the coal stove in the kitchen. It stands within reach of the sleeper in the kitchen corner, and all eight of us share it. The sleeping arrangement assigns Hans and Helga to a couch in the room where we have feasted, the three boys on the bedroom floor, Anna to the couch, and Helene and me to the twin beds. I slide under the big feather coverlet in freshly laundered linen, but I find the mattress so hard that I have to slip one of the gigantic square pillows un-

der me and, thus tucked between soft feathers, reflect grate-
fully that the day could have ended far less satisfactorily.

The night seems too short when Hans calls us for breakfast
and Sunday mass. Once again we are sober and shy and a little suspicious of our accommodations, not knowing the habits and facilities of the house.

"I told you to wait and see," chuckles Helga as I follow
her through the kitchen into a dark hallway, where tools appear to be stored, and through a latched door along a row of
pigsties, where chickens scurry cackling at our approach. At
the end of the dirt walk a tiny, triangular privy is partitioned
off by a swinging door that does not latch. A fresh roll of
tissue is the only concession to modern sanitation. Gingerly
tripping back through the fresh chicken droppings on the
soiled path, we find out that our much needed ablutions must
take place in the same bowl in the kitchen as on the previous
night. The fire is crackling in the stove, and Jerzy's wife,
Basha, with much friendly chatter we cannot understand,
hurries with a steaming kettle to provide fresh water for each
of us. The sleeper from the night before is sitting, fully
dressed in a wrinkled suit and a hat with a turned-up brim,
on top of his dingy bed clothes, ready for church. He is identified as Basha's father. I brush my teeth, sipping water from
my hand and spitting it into a bucket next to the bowl, and
scrub with soap and water the few areas of exposed skin of
face and arms, wondering if the others managed a more thor-
ough cleaning.

A lavish breakfast table is set for us. Jerzy keeps us company, without partaking himself, and urges ever more meat
and bread on us and the fragrant apple cake which Basha
presents on a high-stemmed crystal platter. Tom keeps reaching for yet another hard-boiled egg, telling Jerzy that Basha's
eggs are better than any he has ever eaten. When Jerzy translates this praise, Basha laughs with delight and plants an im-
pulsive kiss on Tom's cheek.

Jerzy rides to church with us while his father-in-law goes
in the car of his son, who is the other man whom we had dis-

turbed at last night's card game and who with his wife and daughter is visiting from the provincial capital.

The drive to church is our first daylight trip through the village. Helene and Anna in the back seat with me whisper comments to each other that will echo repeatedly throughout the following days—muted shouts of recognition and sighs of dismay. But for Jerzy's presence they might have cried out in disgust at the unkempt gardens and the deplorable conditions of the houses we pass. Lacking their precise and nostalgic recollections, I once again marvel at this place I had known as a child, at the sturdy buildings set in typical style of Silesian farms in a square around a courtyard, farm after farm close together along the road, with fields lying out beyond. When we pass Helene's home, I am struck again by the magnitude of the squat two-story house by the creek, reassured that my childhood vision has not betrayed me. And again, like last night in the dark, I am impressed by the size of the rectory and the church that rises from the highest point in the village like the bulwark it had been meant to be. Through the decay of thirty years in the hands of strangers, I see the scenes of childhood vacations, glorying in the discovery of how stately my world once was.

We park again by the rectory. Jerzy, clean-shaven today and sharp-looking in double-breasted suit and tie, is clearly in charge of our party and ushers us into the church. Well-kept on the outside, its interior is beyond reproach as well. I notice with nostalgic amusement that the same narrow, uncomfortable pews have remained. Jerzy did well to hurry us on because few seats are left and we must scatter to find them. Our rotund little pastor reads the mass in full regalia and, much to our surprise, personally takes up the collection. I let myself be carried away by the solemnity of the service. The fervent singing of the congregation captivates me, and I join the refrain in imitation of the melodious foreign sounds whose meaning I can only guess. Behind us a strong male voice stands out, and Helga nudges me and whispers: "That's Jerzy!" I sing along with him with even greater enthusiasm.

I stay behind with Helene who walks slowly up the aisle,

pausing at the side altars and looking at every picture and statue in this church where she was wed and had all of her children baptized. She is lost in thought and unaware of me. With the same silent preoccupation she walks through the old cemetery that surrounds the church, looking for familiar names on weatherworn markers, separating the high weeds that hide them and stepping over fallen trees to find them. This cemetery belongs to the forgotten past, while the new one which the boys discovered beyond the rectory has meaning for today's villagers. There the stones stand straight and polished, many have portraits of the dead imbedded in them, and flowers bloom on the graves.

Our West German license plates have attracted the attention of another family of visitors from the West, and the woman among them identifies herself as one of Hans's relatives whom he had last seen here over thirty years ago.

"Over thirty years" is a recurrent refrain that haunts every conversation. For Anna and Helene it becomes the standard response to a litany of memories as we drive on and they survey and compare and try to seek solace for their laments. Most of the farms sadly show the wear and tear of thirty years' indifferent occupancy, stucco has crumbled from the walls revealing patches of naked brick, some buildings have been left to tumble and decay. Ad nauseam they bemoan the changes from house to house, ignoring Hans's well-meaning interjections:

"Admit that the road is better than it ever was. Don't forget that most of these people are too poor to keep up proper maintenance. They came here with nothing and still have very little."

But Helene is angry at the sight of neglected gardens and windows blind with dirt and broken.

"You would think that in all that time they could have worked harder. Then they wouldn't have so little and live like this."

"Mother, do you know that the bigger places went begging because people shunned them? Many came from very humble conditions where the whole family still slept on the tile stove in the kitchen and the houses were hovels by our standards. Remember, I was over there during the war," explains Hans. "They are still learning to cope with their new country."

The once proud manor house lends credibility to his statement. It looks but a storage shed now, with hardly a pane left in the windows and doors flapping loosely from broken hinges. Villagers strolling in their Sunday best along the road seem content and unmindful of their sad surroundings.

We stop at the house of Anna's parents. Jerzy introduces her to the Polish family who greet her warmly and invite her to roam freely through every room of the house. Only the structure itself is the same because all of the furnishings had been removed or destroyed by looting hordes of Russians and the earliest Polish arrivals before the present settlers came. Over our objections Jerzy insists that all of us are expected inside for cake and coffee. The warm reception has changed Anna's original dismay into more friendly feelings toward the people who now claim her childhood home, and she joins in the talk and laughter that seem to follow Jerzy wherever he goes. He finally breaks off our unscheduled visit with demonstrations of what Basha will do to him for keeping us from her dinner table.

Indeed, it is waiting, and buxom Basha, red-faced from her labors at the hot kitchen stove and perhaps from impatience, can be heard fussing and laughing from the time we pull up at the front door. A platter of homemade noodles is steaming on the table, with a tureen of spicy chicken broth beside it. Though in itself a meal, it is followed by stuffed roast duck and new potatoes laced with cream and brown butter—and on it goes until we recoil from the sight of ever more dishes even though Jerzy relays exhortations from his wife that we have eaten nothing.

Afterwards we explore the village in other directions, accompanied by Helene's and Anna's song of woe, until Hans stops the van at the foot of the so-called parish hill where in times gone by we had taken many Sunday afternoon constitutionals. Tradition survives, and we walk up the slope behind the church as we did then. The path soon becomes narrow and overgrown—it has obviously ceased to be a part of the new village life. From the meadow on top of the hill, where Anna and Helene pick wildflowers, I look to the blue silhouette of the mountain ranges, to where I want to be, and long for tomorrow.

We keep an appointment at the rectory where Hans and Helga unload some of our western treasures while Helene takes a lonely stroll through the large untended garden down the path leading to the edge of her former property. She returns slowly and silently, barely able to be civil to the pastor whom she cannot forgive for the neglect of the once well-kept and productive garden.

The next feast is already laid out for us at his housekeeper's house where the wedding had been celebrated on the previous night. A long, narrow table fills the length of the room, laden with cold meats and relishes. Cakes, some not even sliced into, stand at intervals on long-stemmed platters. The priest presides in a jovial mood and starts the vodka toasts that will be repeated in different versions for hours. Young people drift in by twos and threes, friends and cousins of the bride and groom, so that another table must be set up parallel to ours. They are a handsome, wholesome group, friendly and mannerly, but none prettier than the bride whose soft face is framed by short, dark curls that contrast charmingly with the large blue eyes of a child. Enough of the company speak German so that the din of conversation is bilingual and never ceases. Some of the older men had spent the war years in Germany as deported laborers. They talk about those times freely and seem to have come to terms with their personal history as we, surely, must with ours. The young people speak a hesitant school German that leads to frantic searches for missing vocabulary and lots of laughs.

We sing a traditional toast in German in honor of the newlyweds and are, in turn, treated to a rousing drinking song by the Poles. While the platters are constantly refilled and passed around and our plates loaded if we refuse to partake, the pastor walks up behind the reluctant eaters and drinkers and urges them on, proclaiming himself the guardian angel who blesses food and drink.

The greatest pleasure of this Polish wedding in its second day is for me the company of the happy, confident, beautiful young people. I feel a kinship with them because they belong here as I once belonged. They were born here years after another generation had traded this land in a political game. To them this is home as it is for me.

As we bid farewell all around, I try my few Polish words on one of the handsome boys. He answers effusively, much more than I can understand, and exuberantly kisses my hand in the manner of his elders.

Someone must have observed our discomfiture at the morning toilet. Today the ladies have a bathroom—and that is all it is. Behind a hitherto unnoticed door in the passage between the kitchen and the pigsty lies a tiny room, its length that of an old-fashioned bath tub on ornate legs, its width that of the tub and a tall coal heater. Basha keeps refilling the plastic bowl on a stool in the remaining space, and each of us emerges feeling as elated over this moment of privacy as over the increased measure of cleanliness.

As quickly as we can do justice to an ample breakfast, we drive to one of the larger neighboring communities for the obligatory registration with the authorities. Jerzy comes with us and, through his intercession, two children who also live on the farm. Just how many families reside in the buildings around the farmyard will remain a mystery. A few pieces of candy immediately endear me to the small boy who perches next to me on the edge of the crowded seat, and he leans his blond head against my shoulder.

The administration of the rural area has been established in one of the largest private homes in the community, none other than the haunted house of my relatives. The pale-yellow and white decor of former days has been covered by gray paint. We have noticed that most of the buildings that are painted at all are in that color, indicating most likely lack of choice rather than of taste.

How fortunate for the proud old house to have become a public building and thus be saved! I snap several pictures of it for my aging relatives who will never see it again. Then I sit in a room that I had known and surreptitiously peek through open doors into adjoining ones. They are pleasantly furnished with carpets and potted plants in addition to office furniture. One could live here again, I think for the first time since our arrival in Poland.

The registrars, a middle-aged man and a young girl, peck away on manual typewriters as people file in for documents and information. With Jerzy as our interpreter, the formalities are quickly and pleasantly dispensed with, and a package of British cigarettes for each clerk makes it possible for us to check in and out at the same time, eliminating another report. Jerzy contrives to take me throughout the building, asking idle questions in some offices while I reconnoiter and recollect the rooms' erstwhile appearance.

"Today is your day," says Hans to me as we get ready to leave. "Sit up front with me where you can see better."

And thus the mountains lie in open view before me all the way, growing bigger as we approach them, and at last receive the curvy road into their quiet, climbing woods.

I see the valley open up and wonder if the town below is really my hometown. High-rise apartment blocks at the far edge imbalance the picture in my mind. I want to assign them to a street or identify their location by some landmark, but memory fails me. Entering my hometown as a stranger, I eagerly welcome Hans's suggestion to drive first to the village where I had spent the bitter year after World War II. Now that I am here I bargain for time to postpone the confrontation with the past.

But for the new road that by-passes the bridge across the Biele River, time seems to have stood still in this village of sad memories, or, rather, it has mercilessly taken its toll. I gasp in disgust at the inn where we had lived as refugees; mortar is peeling from the outside walls, the garden a patch of weeds, the magnificent old chestnut tree no longer shades the entrance.

Reluctantly I step into the yard toward the farm buildings. I nod to the untidy woman in the side door of the inn, undecided whether to approach her or flee. Jerzy follows me and through him I explain to the woman what has brought me here. The Polish farmer and his wife whom I had known are long dead; their daughter lives elsewhere in the village, but suddenly I don't want to see her or anyone else. Now the woman opens the door to the main room of the inn, and I recoil from the garish colors, different on each wall, and the disorder within. A broken baby crib stands forlorn in a corner. This is a storage room, the woman says, and during harvest farm hands camp here with their families. Yes, it does look like an abandoned camp. She opens other doors, and I barely perceive the rooms through a haze of memories.

Two small, dirty children peer from the stairway. For a distraction I coax them down with chewing gum and bright ballpoint pens. I turn to leave, but now the woman holds us back and wants to talk. We seem to have unleashed memories of her own. I hand some highly-prized stockings to her and briefly see a smile illuminate her face. When she talks again, her lips begin to quiver and she blinks back tears. Jerzy has stopped translating to listen to her compassionately. For a fraction of a bitter moment, sarcasm poses the question in me whether her tears are for herself or for what she and others have done to us. I shake her hand in hasty farewell and walk quickly to the van.

The woods atop the luscious green slopes beckon to me as they did many years ago, but I turn my back on them to keep from crying, too. Of all the people I remember in this setting, only one person still alive would understand the thoughts and emotions that overwhelm me here. I long to hold Marianne's hand and with her walk up the path into the woods to talk about Nightingale, whose letters I left unanswered when life seemed hopeless and useless, and of Eugen, whose optimistic dreams of regained wealth were shortchanged by reality. Marianne achieved hers of education and money as she had vowed she would; and Annemie, untroubled by a past she has chosen to forget, has the world at her feet as she intended and offers to her children the kind of youth we were denied. How differently our lives turned out which had converged for a last time in this place!

As we take the old road across the bridge to return to town by a different route, the grimy woman we had talked to still stands by her house, mopping her streaming eyes with her apron.

Later Tom asks me: "What did you say to her to make her cry?"

I mumble something about the hard life she must have. How can I explain the tears that well up from the depth of the past to him whose life is yet without a past and its ghosts?

In town we stop at the PKO-store where foreign currency is the only acceptable tender. The small upstairs shop is packed with people among a variety of goods from leather coats to French perfumes and American tooth paste. The liquor counter is besieged by customers. No money changes hands here. The bill is paid at a glass-fronted booth downstairs, and with the receipt the merchandise can then be claimed upstairs.

While we wait by the van for Hans to conclude the cumbersome transaction, a man approaches us to offer inexpensive quarters. The thought of staying overnight in my hometown had already taken hold of my mind and made me pack an overnight bag, but the prospect of any accommodations that the shabby man might have to offer seems discouraging. We lunch at the hotel near the railroad station that now bears the ambitious name "Astoria" and is ranked in Category I, meaning first-class and frequented mostly by foreigners who can afford its rates.

The last time I walked up these marble steps, my best friend Erika and I came here for a farewell drink with two young German officers on their way to the crumbling Russian front—now I can't even recall their faces or their names. My friend is dead and so, perhaps, are they.

Reminiscent of the old days' elegance, the hotel awakens again my desire to spend some time alone here and at my leisure. Hans, who is anxious to leave to pursue his genealogical research in old church records, is in favor of leaving me and picking me up again on the next day. The astronomical price in zloties which we are quoted for the only available room translates into "dirt-cheap" by Hans's calculations in western currency. The women dislike the idea of my staying behind and urge me to reconsider.

Hans hands a bottle to me: "You may need this tonight."

Then my lanky, not usually demonstrative son puts his arm around me.

"Mom, keep this for your protection," he says and slips his precious hunting-knife into my coat pocket.

"I'll cut my finger if I just try to open this thing," I laugh. But my travel companions' implied concern for my safety is contagious and secretly I waver when I see them go. Really, physical harm has not even entered my mind; our encounters with the Polish people so far speak convincingly against that. But without sympathetic companionship I begin to be frightened of my own vulnerability and feel abandoned to my lonely thoughts that must remain unshared.

This is by far the liveliest and noisiest place I have seen in Poland. The passenger station across the square from the hotel explodes with the rattle of trains and loudspeaker announcements every few minutes. The bus station adjacent to it is crowded with people and vehicles, and the traffic through the railroad underpass and across the river bridge never stops. I delve into the din and hustle, knowing exactly where I am going, afraid of what I will find.

I blame the gray sky for the sad, gray relic my town has become. Over the cobblestoned pedestrian crossing that is proclaimed the oldest Gothic bridge in Poland I approach the city hall square and stand stunned at the sight of the naked donjon walls in the background. The blocks of ancient houses and the greenery that used to hide the lower portion of the fortress have been razed. Instead, a walk with some benches at intervals leads to the entrance of the fortress, which seems a tourist attraction now, judging by the number of people strolling toward it. From the upper edge of the square I lose myself into the maze of narrow streets, realizing sadly that even on the sunniest day the dirt and peeling paint on the houses would steep them in gray somberness. On the outskirts a new motel and shopping center momentarily confuse me. I skirt the fortress hill on the pleasant, shady walks of my memories, searching the opposite side of the highway for the old garrison cemetery, then retrace my steps, finally realizing that the park through which a network of pedestrian paths leads to a stark high-rise development is the remnant of the cemetery.

I walk on the widest path that is still flanked by rows of ancient trees and think of the dead soldiers who, perhaps, still lie under the indifferent tufted lawn, forgotten and dishonored. I want to find the spot where Franz was buried and crisscross through the park, always returning to a tree near the center aisle which, in fact or imagination, stirs a faint memory. For a long time I sit on a bench across the highway, unable to leave, ignoring the rain that has begun to fall from the leaden sky. And the drops keep streaming over my face like tears.

Then I roam for what seems like hours on familiar streets, past my school, the houses of friends, down the street where I lived. I stand below the room that for a time Annemie and I had shared with our maid who succeeded Heia. Crazily I wonder if I could still hurl a handful of dirt against the high window as on a winter night long ago. From a dancing party at a friend's farm, the guests from town had been delivered by sleigh to their doorsteps long past midnight, and long past the time when our house door was locked for the night. Counting on our maid's discretion and Mother's sound sleep, I threw dirt against our bedroom window and avoided unpleasant repercussions. Fortunately, Mother did not probe.

Mother, too, is on my mind more than usual. Although I never grew to love her, I made my peace with her, and as an adult came to see her life with sympathetic eyes—her marriage to Father that lasted through six war years and left her widowed, with two less than docile teenagers to contend with and to protect from harm. She lived out her life with Aunt

Gretl's family, comfortably independent on Father's pension, worshipping his memory. As Aunt Gretl had predicted, in one way or another he would always take care of her. Spirited, high-strung Aunt Gretl was reunited with her husband to regain an outwardly normal and active life in a West German city. But by the time she died, her mind had returned entirely to her Silesian past with all its joys and horrors—may she rest in peace at last. Neither she nor Mother revisited the scenes of their happiest and saddest moments to which I am exposing my mind now.

So much is the same, yet everything is different under the pall of age that has been given free reign. Some lots where houses are missing or have been left to tumble down remind me of the gap-toothed mouth of an unsavory derelict. And yet, the residential area is less depressing than the center of town. Beginning with the artless, beflagged cultural palace, a former hotel in which I danced on my first ball under the sparkling chandelier, the shopping streets exude dearth and decay. Kiosks with newspapers, postcards, and sundry trinkets dot the dingy blocks like bright bubbles in a dirty stream. People are darting in and out of small shops with pathetic displays behind unwashed windows. Cabbage, cauliflower, tomatoes, and small green apples seem the only items in ample supply. A few clothing stores offer mediocre merchandise at enormous prices. With somewhat of a shock I recognize that many stores are still trading in the same types of goods as they had over thirty years ago. The hardware store, next to which I had climbed the stairs to visit Heia in the owner's residence, still proclaims "Metal" on a big sign above the window.

For Heia, this place had meant mainly a location close to us; for me, her being here continued to provide me with never-failing love since my birth through the distressing years of my youth. She lived long enough to know my sister and me settled in homes and families of our own and to enjoy my first visit to Germany with the oldest of my sons. She died content, knowing that we no longer needed her, true to her promise to Mama.

Over thirty years ago—the old refrain—the displays were often just as scant after years of wartime austerity, but the store windows were shiny and inviting and the façades proud and cared for. I am beginning to view the crowd as other actors reenacting the frantic search for scarce goods from store to store as in wartime. When I see people queueing outside a store, I can predict that this must be a butcher shop.

I dodge into the parish church out of the gray, dusty bustle and walk through its untarnished splendor with a sense of relief, but I feel too restless to pause for long. At a bakery I buy some sweet rolls for the pittance of three zloties and go by the shortest route to my hotel.

The room with twin beds on opposite walls, a wardrobe, and a table with two chairs is pleasant enough and clean. I feel an urgent need to wash the dirt of the streets off me and do so greedily even though the sink has a piece broken out of the porcelain and no stopper. Then I settle down on the broad window sill to watch the busy railroad square below.

But the sights of the afternoon revolve spookily in my head, mingling with the scenes of long ago, and the contrasts of what I remember and what I have seen are too depressing to bear. I reach for Hans's bottle for solace. The first drink merely intensifies the gloom. What I need is not a sodden nightmare but someone to talk to. Like a prayer, a quotation from Schiller's *Don Carlos* forms on my lips: "*Jetzt gib mir einen Menschen, gute Vorsicht!*"

A few weeks ago I had visited Rudi, my long-ago companion and dancing partner, who had survived the war and remained one of the enduring links to the past. Through pictures and words he had tried to prepare me for this desolate moment, and had warned me that it would be too hard to bear alone. I should have heeded his advice. As the gray day slips into dusk, I feel the long evening threaten me like a promise of torture. I know no one in this foreign town—no one.

No one? Then, out of my conversation with Rudi a name begins to emerge from the recesses of my mind. Although it has the gentlest sound, it cuts like a fanfare through my distress: Pacificus. Without hesitation I respond to the timely cue and cross the bridge toward the monastery, there to ask for a monk by that name. Benches are ranged along the window wall of the wide, quiet corridor toward the monastery garden, and a few people sit there in whispered conversation. So close to the noisy street, there seems to be a hush in here that one hesitates to violate by a normal tone of voice. Even the bell that I press at a window marked *Furta* responds in a muted sound, and I whisper my name and that of the man I want to see to the monk behind the window. Then I wait, sitting apart from the group, assailed by doubts and poised to run.

The wide door at the inside end of the corridor opens and a monk in the brown Franciscan habit smiles my name.

"Pater Pacificus?" I inquire shyly and grasp his outstretched hand.

"You asked to see me? What can I do for you?" His German is as accent-free as mine. It confuses me no less than his direct questions, and I stammer my name and Rudi's name. While he searches his mind for any possible connection between us, he has already closed the door without a sound and invited me to follow him into a visitor's room.

It is so easy to talk to his serene, open face that my words tumble out in a rush, explaining what has brought me to this town, mixing the past and the present. He gets the idea.

"And you find everything changed more than you expected."

The simple statement that shows his understanding of my agitated state breaks the sharp, accusatory point off the bitterness I had meant to conceal from him. Under his soothing questioning he lets me sketch a picture of my life in this very town. I am amazed how much he knows, as if he had been one of us a long time ago, and how interested he is in its history. He excuses himself to return with a briefcase full of maps and brochures, chattering away like an old acquaintance and filling me in on the fates of some of the clergy and nuns who were part of my childhood.

A gentle rap on the door admits a serving girl with a dinner tray, and he insists that I eat the tasty simple meal and keeps refilling my cup with hot, sweet lemon tea.

Imperceptively the conversation has turned away from the past to the Polish present. As a Pole he cannot be entirely objective, but as a priest he stands outside the political shifts and talks with a measure of detachment, yet with empathy, about the hard life in present-day Poland. Later I will discover the precarious balance between Catholicism and political power that exists here as nowhere else in the world.

For the first time I experience a semblance of understanding the conditions which I have observed. He tells me how the settlers, themselves made homeless in eastern Poland, came to this land that had been exploited by the Russians and the first radical elements among their own people, how they felt that they were living a temporary reprieve that might be terminated at any time by the returning German natives. They had neither the will nor the means to maintain or rebuild, and they coped with chronic shortages as best they could. Only when West German Chancellor Willy Brandt confirmed the Potsdam Agreement in the early seventies did they take heart and begin to feel permanently at home. Thus what little rebuilding and renovation we had seen was as yet of too recent a vintage to catch up with the decay and neglect of decades. In the midst of uncertainty and hardships, the people nevertheless and all the more clung to their traditionally fervent religious faith, beautified the churches out of their poverty, and confounded the Communist regime. Their true national hero is the primate of Poland, Cardinal Wyszynski, the fearless, grand old man.

"Think of it as an elephant hunt," explains Pater Pacificus. "He does not have political or military power to fight the government, but he can make a lot of noise, just like the elephant hunter may scare the monster with crackling and rattling sounds when his rifle is useless. Then the people rally behind the cardinal and make a row that makes the politicians quake and walk more softly for a while."

Not only the dignitaries of the church but even he, a humble monk, enjoys the respect of the people and certain privileges. He guesses correctly that I am staying at a Category I hotel and how much I pay for a room.

"That price is the official one for foreigners. A Polish guest would probably pay half that price, but at the sight of my robe it may drop down to a tenth," he chuckles.

I learn of the plight of the working people who have the wherewithal for a very simple existence—I remember how little I paid at the bakery—but struggle for, perhaps never attain, any comforts beyond the barest necessities. Exports are meant to fill the coffers of the Polish state; even things that are most of all needed here are exported. Will I ever taste a Polish sausage again without recalling the long lines at the butcher shops?

The example of a Polish working woman who would have to spend a month's wages for a pound of coffee and a ham makes me realize how far my definition of luxuries is removed from hers.

As if to atone for his departure from my personal concerns, the monk excuses himself again and returns to spread a veritable library of books about this area on the table for my inspection, insisting that I compile a bibliography right then and there so that I can purchase some of them later.

"All of these you can take with you," he says as he sets aside picture postcards and other mementos and warms once more to tales of history and anecdotes about my home. He talks enthusiastically about the monastery church, a baroque treasure, which I have so far neglected to visit, and invites me to the solemn high mass next morning on the prior's feast day.

I feel overwhelmed by his touching humanity and generosity, by the twinkling good humor of his lively conversation. I had come to this stranger with a heavy, reproachful heart, and he has succeeded in opening my eyes and soothing me into a conciliatory, reflective mood. In my heart I beg forgiveness for all of my harsh, uncharitable judgments born of selfishness and ignorance.

From the depth of my bag I gather the remaining packages of chewing gum and, with some embarrassment, precious pantyhose for the kitchen help, and remember in time to add a nest egg for him personally for a trip west. Once before, with the help of a prelate I knew well, he had managed to join my expelled countrymen for their annual reunion and pilgrimage to a Westphalian shrine. His beaming pleasure shames me.

Hours have passed unnoticed, and it has gotten quite dark outside.

"One more thing I must show you before you leave," says Pater Pacificus, taking me through the silent halls to the refectory. One half of the tall-ceilinged, vaulted room is obscured by scaffolding. When the light is turned on, I see the expanse of white-clothed tables in the other half and above them ceiling frescoes in vibrant colors. The hand of a master craftsman has removed the dust and grime with bread to restore them to their original beauty, and the result is all the more striking for seeing the uncompleted work in comparison.

On this aesthetically upbeat note I take my leave. When I thank my host in an insufficient formula for his delightful companionship, he shakes his head and takes my hand in his: "May God repay you."

For what, my friend, I think, too moved to say the words—you have saved me from despair in this my soul's dark night.

Sleep fails me. While I wrestle in solitude once more with all I have seen and heard that day, the traffic bangs and rattles unabated under my window, and I long for the peaceful remoteness of the monastery.

My watch has stopped. With sheer luck or intuition I arrive at the monastery church in time for the high mass. A priest is just concluding a service at the altar when I enter, and as he faces the congregation for the final blessing, I recognize with a start my friend of last evening and feel truly blessed.

Then the bell rings for the beginning of the high mass. The church is glorious in the reflection of electric lights on white and gold sculpture and the glow of candles and flowers at the altar. The fragrance of incense drifts my way as in times before the simplification of Catholic ritual. Three priests at the high altar, resplendent in gold-embroidered robes, intone the chants in resonant voices. The congregation's responses are led by a few habited young monks in the front pews. They all sing with strength and fervor, leaving me alone silent in frustration, only able to listen with exquisite pleasure.

A woman slides into the pew next to me, placing an enamel jug of milk on the seat between us, and this incongruous gesture in a house of worship seems symbolic of the natural integration of religion and her workaday life. In my thoughts I thank my friend for bringing me to this place at this hour to witness the steadfast and defiant faith of a people I am beginning to view with a kind of love.

The hotel dining room is occupied by a German-speaking group of tourists whose guide has difficulty hastening them from the tables to their waiting bus. When even the tardiest stragglers have left, a young couple and I, seated far apart, have the room to ourselves. My solitary breakfast consists of a piece of fried sausage, bread and butter, a few slices of tomatoes, and coffee served in the customary glass with the grounds settled in the bottom third. I drink it sparingly, savoring the clearest liquid from the top and gingerly extracting the last drops from the murky sediment. A young cleaning-girl comes with mop and pail from the region of the bar and goes to work on the marble floor, progressing to my irritated amusement to within inches of my feet.

Later while readying my overnight bag I listen to a radio newscast. The German reporter speaks of quotas and agricultural achievements, leaving no doubt in my mind that I am tuned to an East German station.

The streets are again bustling with people and traffic when I leave the hotel to explore the town in other directions than on the previous day. From a new shopping center I pass through a park in which a bright yellow monument proclaims the glory of the Soviet army. Within sight of the monastery downstream I discover a new bridge. A narrow, hard-trodden path leads to it over heaps of construction dirt overgrown with grass. The bridge, without railings, is as wide as a two-lane road, its surface concrete marked with footprints, and ends abruptly on the opposite bank where I must jump across a gap to the path continuing on yet more old construction dirt. An unfinished project of old vintage that calls to mind other building sites we have seen where the growth of whole housing developments seemed to have been stultified in a state of near completion.

Elsewhere crowds of people pass in and out of the gate to a fenced-in area. I join the throng and find myself milling along through an open-air market. Booths offer crocheted lacework, used clothing, row upon row of shoes—few new ones, most are well-worn and lacking necessary laces. In between the booths are small enterprises selling produce out of burlap bags and glass jars; some seem to have mere handfuls spread for sale on the asphalt. An old woman in antiquated apparel, scarf tied low over her face, squats on a low stool amid jars of berries, toothlessly chewing a wad of tobacco. While she is concluding business with a customer, she flips her skirt up and begins digging money from a coarse knit stocking tucked in her muddy boot.

Here and at street corners everywhere vendors offer some kind of colored drink, perhaps fruit juice, from pushcarts. Once again I pass through the business area, incredibly alive with activity but dirty and pathetic in its offerings. Occasionally, bright printed ribbons and placards provide a splash of color in the eternal gray, and I wonder what cheerful messages they bear.

I wander along a street between blocks of apartment buildings. Now and then gapes a space filled with the rubble of a former house. Through gates that open to tunneled underpasses into backyards, I spy darkness and filth. Even here the traffic thunders past intermittently, especially heavy trucks that belch vile-smelling, sooty fumes—what kind of fuel are they burning? A light breeze constantly stirs up the dust and litter at my feet until I feel so sickened from the smells and dirt and noise that I backtrack hastily through this unpleasantness. Even my kindlier attitude toward the people who live here now cannot alter the fact that this has little resemblance to the place I had known so well and came to find again.

To Lose a War

My sentimental quest for my hometown is over. I have been walking the streets of Kłodzko, Poland. Glatz has ceased to exist save in my memories.

With disgust and resolute denial, I scrub the real and imagined residue of my morning walk off my body, wishing to cleanse my mind as well, and impatiently watch the hotel driveway for the bright van to rescue me.

We take a long drive through villages and resorts away from town. Hans administers aspirins and lots of fruit juice to me along the way to restore my obviously lacking vitality. By the time my splitting headache subsides, we have gained a mountain road, and through breaks in the thick foliage we see small settlements dotting the valley, and flashes of sunlight illuminate slopes and mountain passes in visions as lovely as memory.

Jerzy greets us in the farmyard in his usual expansive style, but his questions about my solitary adventure turn to shouts of woe.

"What is? Something wrong? Oh, you are sick!" he cries and leads me to Basha's waiting table.

Jerzy watches over the health and well-being and good spirits of all of us. He knows a remedy for everything; when all else fails, a glass of vodka helps to soothe the pain.

During my absence Tom has cut a deep gash into his thumb. After managing to stem the flow of blood by winding a handkerchief around it tightly, he goes about asking for conventional first aid. Jerzy lops a shoot off a cactus on the window sill, splits it lengthwise and presses the cut side on the wound. Swearing that it will heal within two days without leaving a scar, he wraps a strip of green utility tape around the thumb. Everyone is dubious of the result but willing to put faith in Jerzy.

Hans has developed an annoying irritation of the eyes. Jerzy the healer is at hand with a paste of yeast and milk which Hans distastefully plasters over his eyes at night. Hans and Helga spend a slightly nauseated night from sniffing the unpleasant sour odor, but when Hans rinses the risen and caked yeast off in the morning, his eyes look fresh and clear.

We are learning not to make fun of Jerzy's home cures because they really work.

A chilly wind has risen in the evening, and the boys and Jerzy rush to get the cattle from the pasture back into the stable. The windows flap and rattle until we must close them against the growing storm. The boys remember to dismantle their tent in the garden, where they have been sleeping after the first night, before it is torn off its moorings.

Once again we sit around the table and Jerzy introduces us to his specialty, pure alcohol mixed with honey from his thirty bee hives. Though far from being a nectar for the gods, it slides down more easily with every swig, and we daren't refuse our host's brew. Basha is now joining us in the late evenings, bursting with robust vitality and good humor. While Hans and Jerzy with their irreverent and witty banter keep us laughing, Basha in frustration interrupts with countless impatient "what?"s in Polish and then shakes with hilarity like the rest of us when Jerzy takes time to translate. Since the first day, all talk about moving to the rectory as originally planned has been abandoned because Jerzy and Basha simply refuse to let us go.

The storm gusts and howls on, and suddenly we sit in darkness. Jerzy has candles within reach—power outages seem to be nothing unusual—and places a few on our table. He takes others upstairs to an apartment where our boys have discovered some teenage girls with whom they communicate in a jumble of languages and presumably more non-verbal sharing. By midnight the lights flash on again, and we acknowledge them almost with regret.

Somehow Hans finds time for tracking down ancestors in the parish records and for helping Helga distribute the clothing and canned goods that we carried in the van's baggage area. One family of happy recipients is so overjoyed at their good fortune that they shower us with artwork that one of the talented sons produces in abundance.

A plaster of Paris plaque depicting the village church catches Tom's eye, and he must have it. Cast into its circular edge is the Polish name of the village, a name we are not likely to forget.

In addition to the gifts, Hans urges us to select other paintings not so much for their aesthetic value but to justify a gift of money which the family can accept with grace.

A cold, rainy morning finds us on the road once again more for my sake than any of the others', bound for an industrial city in which I had lived for a few years as a child. The previous night's devastating storm has left signs everywhere in the countryside, toppled trees, broken limbs, ripe grain flattened on the ground.

Hans interprets the names at the entrance to towns, now and then pointing to unmistakable landmarks to keep me better oriented.

There is no mistaking the outskirts of Wałbrzych, an ugly, sooty coal center. Wet with rain, it looks blacker than ever. More rapidly than I had expected we find the center of oldtown and pull into an alley to park. Maneuvering the van into position, Hans backs into a small car behind us, and we cringe at the sound of breaking glass. We hear a woman lamenting loudly and our helpless, embarrassed captain trying to calm her by tone of voice rather than impotent German words. Out of nowhere a man appears to act as interpreter. A pack of cigarettes for his invaluable services and western money for the woman to cover more than the minor damage to her car spare us the interference of the police, which would have meant an unscheduled delay at best.

Because it is expected of me, I take a stroll over drenched streets to the parish church to look once again at the tall Gothic stained-glass windows and up to the choir loft where eons ago I swung from the ropes with the sacristan's children while tolling the bells for the Angelus. I pass our apartment building, dismayed at the concrete strip across the walk where Father had rented a fenced-in patch of lawn for our very own playground, and by my brothers' school and Father's office. My heart never clung to this city, and there is nothing here to endear it to me now.

Through a network of new roads we find our way to a nearby resort, just far enough away to escape the grimy atmosphere of Wałbrzych. And here, at the sight of the house where I was born, I find my earliest memories confirmed. Even in its decay the once lovely building stands high and stately, although the broad steps to the terrace are broken off and the gap filled with concrete blocks, wash flapping in the wet wind on the erstwhile terrace and the garden a jungle of weeds and untrimmed bushes. What a magic place it had been long ago!

Hans has promised Helga a day in the Giant Mountains if she would consent to come along on this trip. To minimize the risk of finding ourselves without lodging a second time, we take an inordinately long roundabout way home, in order to reserve rooms for the next night in a hotel high in the mountains. The winding approach, in spite of the on-and-off showers, reveals the kind of mountain vistas I love, and I wish we were not only passing through at this time.

In a town through which we have driven on several occasions without stopping, Helene pleads for time to visit a church of old Cistercian origin. When we pause there on our return trip, I steal a few solitary minutes for a stroll to the local cemetery where Mama was buried when I was a young child. Although I still know the spot where her grave ought to be, I search for it in vain. The stones immortalize a generation of more recent dead, and none of the few remaining old markers bears her name. Now I know that not even graves—not my mother's, not my brother's—bind me to this land any more. A strange sense of bitter relief infuses my sadness as I turn my back on yet another place that has lost its meaning for me. Hans comes walking towards me as if divining a new sorrow; he does not want to abandon me a second time after witnessing the effect of my lonely visit to my hometown.

Our announcement that we will leave in the morning is shouted down harshly by Jerzy and disapproved in excited Polish by his wife. They simply refuse to believe that we mean it.

Unbeknownst to us, they had earlier in the week dispatched their visiting niece on a foraging trip to Wrocław. The child had left on a train at dawn to arrive there to line up for meat by the time the stores opened, and she had returned on the evening train with a supply of all kinds of sausage to supplement the home-butchered meat supply. Jerzy had mentioned before that in the provincial capital and in some industrial cities it is easier to obtain meat because the hardworking populace is apt to strike if food becomes scarce. He routinely makes a trip to the Upper Silesian coal-mining area to stock up every few weeks. There is no butcher in any of the nearby villages, and we had seen for ourselves the queues at meat markets in area towns.

And now, he complains, we aren't staying to share their bounty! This is the first note of discord we have heard during all the light-hearted hours in his company.

We sit deep into the night with him and Basha, sipping his potent homemade brew, and speculate on our next meeting. Hans persuades him to promise a visit in the west and, in his turn, gives his solemn word always to take lodging at Jerzy's house whenever he comes to this area of Poland. We pay tribute to Basha's cuisine by asking for some of her excellent recipes that we have sampled during our stay. Jerzy's laborious translation in this to him unfamiliar and uninteresting subject produces a strange list of ingredients and instructions on which we will surely have to improvise according to our housewifely instincts.

Other questions that have been building up in us during the week receive clearer and more reliable answers from him, for instance, the striking difference between the huge collective fields in East Germany and the traditional patchy look we have observed in the Polish countryside. Who owns the land here? The state or individuals, Jerzy tells us, and recently the state has begun lending substantial amounts of money on long-term loans, and foregoing repayment and interest in the first few years, to encourage private ownership of farm land. The reckoning comes at retirement age: A private farmer has no claim on the state-paid old-age pension; only those who have worked the land for the state without purchasing it are entitled to a pension. The best of both options can be achieved by combining them: Acquire property early in life and make the most of it, then sell it to the state to ensure a carefree old age.

Jerzy chuckles: "If I could be born again, do you know what I would want to be?" His eyes sparkle and twinkle with mischief. "A gypsy. Gypsy man is happy and lazy. Gypsy woman works and cares for him."

We tease him saying that he is living that way now.

At that he recites his share of the work: "I have my bees, I take care of the animals, pick berries for Basha, and I work a little in the fields. You know—" and he starts to rise to show us again as on the first evening the surgical scar on his back that excuses him from heavy labor. He was a railroad conductor until his disability retirement and marriage to Basha, whose father owned the farm. He still carries his railroad pass and proudly displays it for us to admire his younger good looks.

"Jerzy, is this your birthday?" Helga points to one of the dates on his identification card. "It's the same as mine!"

A bear hug and a kiss from Jerzy seal the bond of this joyous coincidence, and we must toast the lucky sign of their birth.

Secretly Hans has set up the tape recorder to preserve the sound of Jerzy's voice and laughter which have happily underscored our hours in his house and struck a balance against the sad moments we experienced elsewhere. When Jerzy hears a familiar voice in the room when no one is talking, he is for once at a loss for words and then laughingly chides Hans for being a spy before continuing, unabashed, to entertain us with his lively talk.

The morning of our departure begins with a round of visits to the pastor and others who have made us feel welcome in their homes like lifetime friends. Jerzy and Basha, tears trickling down their faces, give men and women alike affectionate triple kisses of farewell. Even Helene, who has remained more aloof and unreconciled than any of us, walks away with quivering lips to hide her emotion.

The van is once again loaded to capacity, with travel provisions from our hosts, jars of Jerzy's honey for each of us, roots with soil packed around them for Helga's garden at home, the paintings and other gifts that were showered upon us wherever we went. Homeless strangers when we arrived less than a week ago, we leave behind us people we will never forget.

Hans and Werner have planned the route to take us by a music store in a city we had passed through once before. Werner's heart is set on a new trumpet that is priced in the thousands of zloties. An idle passer-by follows them into the store to enter the negotiations as interpreter. When he conveys to the proprietor that these customers consider paying in West German currency, the transaction is moved to an adjoining private office and concluded—in terms of our monetary values—at a bargain price that makes everyone a winner.

The sky that had already loosened two hailstorms on us brightens more and more as we follow the winding road into the mountains, occasional sunshine caressing the peaceful, dreamy fields and meadows that drop farther and farther below in the distance. The timeless charm of the wooded mountain ranges touches me with homesickness on this day of farewell.

Karpacz stretches on a steep incline up toward the highest peak of the Giant Mountains. Leisurely strolling crowds mark it as the favorite vacation spot it has always been. Our hotel lies even above the resort as near the summit as the road will take us. We hurriedly take the most essential baggage to our three rooms. Helene, Anna, and I share a room with garish decor in orange and bright red, but its spaciousness and comfortable furnishings are a pleasant surprise.

The woods that rise steeply at the rear of the lodge beckon irresistibly. A five-minute walk away lies the cable-car station, and we join the throng of tourists lined up for the ride. The babble of sounds around is us composed of Polish,

Epilogue

Czech, and German, with Tom adding a definite minority in
English. When Hans pays the fare for all of us, it amounts
to a fraction of one person's ticket for a cable-car ride in
the Alps.

"Well," he comments drily under his breath, "there you
have an example of how a Socialist state spoils its devoted
citizens."

Single chair seats that have to be caught in motion carry
us above the tree tops in sparkling sunshine. As the long ride
carries us higher and higher into regions often shrouded in
dense fog and clouds, and an icy breeze rocks the seats, the
barren nudity of the summit remains sharply etched against
the flawless sky. Chilled through and through, we drop onto
the landing platform to enjoy the miracle of a picture-
postcard view far into the Silesian valleys.

Helga, a child of the flatlands, gasps at the beauty spread
before us: "From up here your Silesia still looks every bit as
good as in your tales." And as a sobering afterthought she
adds: "Much better than below."

The boys are already far ahead of us on the stony path
across the plateau that leads toward the sudden steep ascent
to the summit. Helga and I follow them more slowly, feeling
the thin, cold air stab at our lungs.

"How much longer to the top?" we ask a group of young
soldiers sitting on a bench. They make signs with their hands
and laugh at our futile guessing game.

The boys come trotting back to us, shouting that we cannot go on. At the base of the last steep climb they have been
stopped by armed guards who permit only Poles and Czechs
to pass, not even East German citizens, and a group of these
just reaches us, giving vent to their undisguised displeasure.
The border splits the mountain top in two between Poland
and Czechoslovakia. Here we stand just below the old Silesian and Bohemian summit lodges and the weather and radar
stations and are denied a yet more glorious view, cheated out
of the satisfaction of conquering the peak. But the slow de-
scent by cable car keeps the lovely panorama before us for a
long time until the tall evergreens block the view.

In the evening we sit together in one of the rooms. Hans sets a bottle of vodka on the table and turns on the tape recorder. Jerzy comes alive in the sound of his witty fractured comments and happy laughter and is with us once more.

The rainy morning hides the mountain world behind a dark, impenetrable screen. Nevertheless we pass groups of tourists on their morning outing.

"Whether rain or shine, the Socialist vacationer must follow his daily program and enjoy it," remarks Hans sarcastically.

Now that we are headed west once more, we are in a hurry to get home, stopping only briefly along the highway to buy baskets of wild blueberries from children who flag us down. Two Russian soldiers at wood's edge across the road laugh out loud at the excited bargaining of the waifs and their scramble for what little candy and gum we give them to share.

I approach the border with misgivings, but Hans allays my fears: "Don't worry, our tormentor won't be there. These people are rotated every few days to keep them from getting too well acquainted with each other or any particular stretch of border. Trust is not a mark of the Communist regime."

Thus reassured, I enjoy a shopping spree among the crystal offerings in the duty-free shop.

We cross all checkpoints with delays because of heavy weekend traffic but without unpleasant incidents. An East German guard who inquires politely where we have been comments on that beautiful countryside where he, too, would like to spend a vacation. More uniformed personnel seem to be on duty than before.

"Believe it or not," one wit informs me, "in this country of seventeen million it takes one half to guard the other half, and half of that is over sixty-five." My traveling companions hold no love for our erstwhile countrymen and their methods of keeping everyone in line.

At the entrance to West Germany a relaxed border guard glances at our passports and waves us on:

"A whole bunch back from Poland! It's not worth checking you—you are allowed to carry everything under the sun with you anyway."

That night at Hans's home we sit long at the cozy bar in the family room and celebrate our return to the frail freedom and affluence that is ours to enjoy once again, and we cherish them more consciously for having experienced their absence. But the thought of Jerzy and the others whom we left behind borders that mark much more than a line between neighboring countries hangs over us like guilt. Theirs is a life, like ours in wartime, of shortages and political tension, never free of the threat of even worse conditions. They, too, at least those our age and older, have experienced displacement from their homes and hardships in establishing new lives. Perhaps, there are more common bonds between them and us than we could recognize in the postwar upheaval and violence—we were victimized, all of us, and they still are.

"Just for a moment," I challenge Hans, "try to imagine what our lives would be like if we had not been expelled after the war."

"If you had asked my mother that question, she would have told you that it would look a lot better there than it does now," he laughs. "Personally," he adds soberly, "I think they may actually have done us a favor by throwing us out. My life now couldn't be better."

Unless, I can't keep from reflecting sadly, Silesia had remained German, but the thought is without bitterness.

Helga and I spend the next day washing our travel clothes. Rolf is brushing his teeth in the bathroom when we enter with some hand laundry.

"Mama, what's that awful smell?" he shakes himself. We laugh together, remembering the minimal hygiene during a week away from bath tubs and other luxurious contraptions. By nightfall all traces have been removed of the most unusual vacation we ever shared.

No one has suffered any ill effects from it except Rolf's canary. It lies dead in its cage from want of customary care.

The boys prepare a ceremonious burial in the flower garden for this innocent victim of our trip, and over the grave Werner blows a rousing military salute on his brand-new Polish trumpet.

Every life is unique to the one who lives it and yet each of us is a cloned victim of times and circumstances shared with many others.

These particular stories unfolded in a time and place all but forgotten by many and never known by many, many more. They are meant neither as an indictment nor an apology nor melodrama. They are merely personal experiential variations on a universal theme that is played over and over. Dates and localities may change—from Europe in the forties to Asia in the sixties, to Africa in the seventies—individual destinies parallel themselves endlessly through the centuries all over the world. The Trail of Tears which the American Indians trod encircles the globe, never reaching its final destination.

These stories are neither unique nor spectacular: They are offered in a small voice raised by one from among the many homeless and uprooted, anywhere, everywhere. May they persuade those who have homes and love to cherish these treasures and realize their transience.